southwest
MODERN

From Marfa to New Mexico:
18 TRAVEL-INSPIRED QUILTS

Kristi Schroeder

Published in 2017 by Lucky Spool Media, LLC
www.luckyspool.com
info@luckyspool.com

Text © Kristi Schroeder
Editor: Susanne Woods
Design: Page + Pixel
Illustrator: Courtney Kyle
Photographs by: Kurt Griesbach
(unless otherwise noted)

Photographs by Page + Pixel on pages 9, 15, 41
and 115

9 8 7 6 5 4 3 2 1
First Edition
Printed in China

Library of Congress Cataloging-in-Publication
Data available upon request

ISBN: 978-1-940655-28-4

Dedication

For my parents. Your endless love, support,
and words of encouragement have made me
the creative that I am today.

Table of Contents

Introduction

Truth be told, I fell into the quilting world quite accidentally. I spent my early twenties to mid-thirties working as a graphic designer in the corporate world, specializing in design, advertising, and in-house branding. I lived in Austin, Chicago, San Francisco, and Dallas, and recently returned to Austin. While working in Dallas, I craved a creative outlet that didn't involve sitting in front of a computer. Soon, I discovered a modern fabric store called CityCraft that had the most amazing fabrics and offered sewing classes. Honestly, it was the fabrics that did it for me in the beginning. I just fell in love with them and felt like I had to make something with them. I signed up for a beginner quilting class, learned the ins and outs of piecing and quilting, and was instantly hooked—much to my mother's delight. She had been trying for years to get me in front of a sewing machine (moms know best, y'all!). Shortly thereafter I found myself designing my own quilt patterns (with lots of trial and error) and gifting quilts to friends and family.

Fast forward six years, and I was designing in-house for the luxury retailer Neiman Marcus—my absolute dream job, as I love all things fashion—but I found myself burned out creatively. I decided to take time off to regroup and figure out what I truly wanted out of life. I loved being a designer and loved the tactile aspects of sewing/quilting—from picking out the fabric to cutting and piecing it all back together again. Creating something from a design in my head that I could touch and feel made me insanely happy. In August 2014, I decided it was the perfect time to take the entrepreneurial plunge and I launched Initial K Studio, Modern Quilts by Design.

Like most artists and quilters, a lot of the inspiration for my patterns and designs occurs when I'm traveling or exploring the great

outdoors. A few summers ago, I had a chance to venture to West Texas for a girls' birthday trip. I had just finished writing my Arrowhead pattern and, at the last minute, decided to take one of my sample quilts to photograph. I took my time capturing the quilt in as many different environments as possible as we explored Marathon, Big Bend, and Marfa. While I was traveling, ideas for new quilt patterns began percolating. What if I created a collection of quilt patterns that represented my passion for both travel and design? It made perfect sense—my design shop was founded on the basis of travel as inspiration.

Why Focus on the Southwest?

As a native Texan, I love everything about this state. It's where I grew up. From the lapping waves along the south Texas coast to the expansive vistas of West Texas, all of Texas is beautiful to me. As for New Mexico, I have family ties to Pecos and spent most every summer enjoying the mountain views there. It's the place where I disconnect from the world and recharge while hiking the trails and taking in the mountain air. From the mountain ranges to the rich Native American culture of Santa Fe, the state is filled with never-ending sources of inspiration.

I will say that this new chapter of my life— quitting my job, starting my own business—has been a roller coaster ride. But I wake up each morning with a sense of excitement about what the day will hold. I hope you get a sense of that while exploring this book. Not only do I want to motivate you to create my quilts using your own fabrics, but I hope you consider visiting the places that inspired my designs. After all, this a travel book of quilt inspiration that appeals to quilters and non-quilters alike who have a love for travel, design, and adventure.

Inspiration, Design Process and Building a Color Palette

Inspiration

I find the majority of the inspiration for my designs while traveling or exploring the great outdoors. From the colors of a stone paved walkway in Santa Fe to a stained-glass window found in the Rijksmuseum in Amsterdam, inspiration is everywhere. When something catches my eye, I quickly snap a picture with my camera phone to refer to later. I certainly encourage you to do the same! Perhaps the next time you're on your way to work, you'll notice a repeating tile pattern in the subway walls or take note of a color combination in the fabric of a fashionable dress in a shop window. The key to gathering inspiration from anywhere is to challenge yourself to view everyday objects and places in a different light.

My Design Process

When starting a new project, part of my creative process is to assemble a mood/inspiration board in the studio as well as a secret Pinterest board. For me, this is the most fun part of beginning a new project. I pin anything and everything from my collection of camera phone images, old postcards, and/or pages ripped out of a magazine until, eventually, a design story begins to emerge. From there, I move forward with sketching various design ideas in my notebook. Some sketches are great and others ... not so much. That's just fine by me. It's best to just put the pencil to the paper and let it all go. I do find it helpful to reference my inspiration board as I sketch. This ensures that I'm on the right track with executing my original design vision. Next, I transfer my favorite design ideas into a computer program and continue to refine the sketch to make it suitable for piecing. Once I'm happy with the design, I begin my second favorite part of the design process ... adding color!

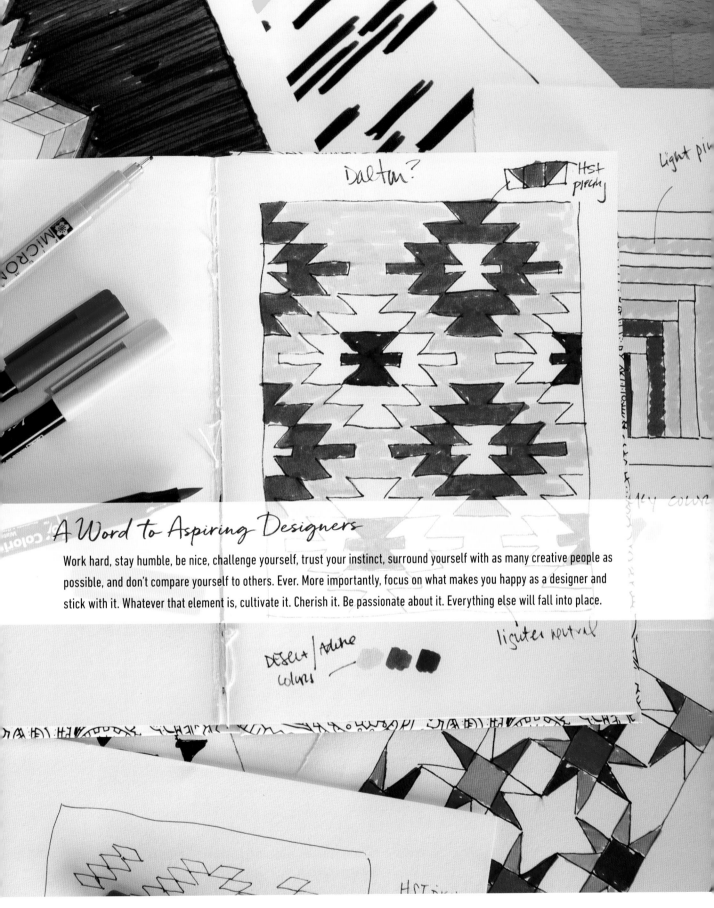

A Word to Aspiring Designers

Work hard, stay humble, be nice, challenge yourself, trust your instinct, surround yourself with as many creative people as possible, and don't compare yourself to others. Ever. More importantly, focus on what makes you happy as a designer and stick with it. Whatever that element is, cultivate it. Cherish it. Be passionate about it. Everything else will fall into place.

Building a Color Palette

I absolutely love color. Some
find color intimidating, but
if you go with what you like,
it's difficult to go wrong. Try
cutting up fabric color cards
or paint cards, then mix them
all up and see what happens.
The various accidental happy
fabric combinations will
surprise you. If you are still
unsure what colors to use for a
project, I suggest referencing
a painting from your favorite
artist or perhaps a favorite
scarf hanging in your closet and
begin building a color palette
from there. Most designers
refer to this method as "color
chipping." For example, for the
Zia mini (see page 92), I looked
to my collection of turquoise
jewelry for inspiration.

The design and color palette of
the Wanderlust quilt (see page
56) were inspired by the eclectic
vibe and bright colors of a
vintage trailer. Don't be afraid
to experiment with various
color combinations. The more
you work with color, the more
you'll learn about what colors
work best for you through trial
and error. The possibilities are
endless, y'all.

1039 BORDEAUX   481 SANGRIA   451 VALENTINE   1049 BRT. PINK   1225 MED. PINK

Piecing and Quilting How-To

I love, love, love the beginning of a new quilt project and all the challenges that come along with it. Are the dimensions right? Will the colors come together? Is the design working? Much of this involves making decisions as I progress, but it is all backed up by my go-to tools of the trade and the sewing tips that I've developed over the years. If you are new to quilting, I highly recommend joining your local quilt guild—modern or traditional. No matter your design aesthetic, you'll meet the most amazing quilters who are chock full of knowledge. You can also find a free PDF of Quilt Making Basics on the www.luckyspool.com website.

Tools of the Trade

My sewing arsenal includes:

45mm rotary cutter with replacement blades

Self-healing 24″ × 36″ cutting mat

Omnigrid rulers: 6½″ × 24″, 6½″ × 12″, and a 10½″ square

Kai scissors

Seam ripper

Dritz flower head pins

Dritz curved quilting pins

Painter's tape

Washi tape

Sticky notes

Fabric marking pencil and/or pen

505 Spray and Fix adhesive

Mary Ellen's Best Press starch alternative

Iron

Ironing board with a 22″ × 59″ surface (see Resources)

Aurifil 50-weight thread

Shout color catchers

FABRIC PREP

When starting a project, I prefer not to pre-wash my fabric and instead I starch and iron it until it is wrinkle-free. I find that my cuts are more accurate if I use a starch alternative to stabilize my fabric and provide some body. As soon as I finish ironing each piece, I use a fine-tip permanent marker to label the fabric color along the selvage. This helps to keep track of the different colors and is especially helpful when working with neutrals.

I keep a stack of sticky notes on hand too. As I cut each fabric according to my cutting directions, I make a note of the finished size of each cut and subcut. This method keeps me organized, eliminates the guesswork of determining individual cuts (especially when some are so similar), and helps me stay on track as I'm piecing.

Stitch Length

When piecing fabric, my general rule of thumb is to use a 2.0mm machine stitch length and a fresh universal 80/12 needle in my machine. When I am quilting with a walking foot, I like to increase my stitch length to 3.5mm.

Seam Allowance

When it comes to determining the seam allowance in piecing, a ¼" seam is the standard. Most newer sewing machines provide a ¼" seam attachment as well as a ¼" mark on the throat plate. If you have an older machine, like my Singer Featherweight (my go-to sewing machine when traveling), you can use washi tape to create your own ¼" guide.

Pressing

Press seams to one side or press them open? That was my first question when I was in the early stages of learning to piece a quilt top. I have experimented with both methods over the years and my favorite method is to press the seams open unless I am paper piecing. I like to first spray the seams using a starch alternative and then press the seams open with a hot, dry iron (no steam setting!). The end result? My seams lay flat, and in my opinion, aligning the quilt block seams is easier than trying to nest the seams together. Experiment with both pressing methods to discover which you prefer.

Assembling Half-Square Triangles (HSTs)

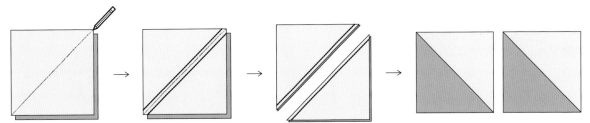

Figure 1

1. Using a fabric marking pen and a ruler, draw a diagonal line on the wrong side of one Half-Square Triangle (HST) square.

2. Position the marked square and the second HST square right sides together and pin in place. Sew a ¼″ seam on either side of the marked line from Step 1. Using a ruler and rotary cutter, cut along the marked line to create two HST units (Fig. 1). Press the seams open.

Assembling Half-Rectangle Triangles (HRTs)

1. Referencing the diagram adjacent and using a fabric marking pen and a ruler, on the *wrong* side of a Fabric 1 rectangle, mark a dot ½″ away from both raw edges of the bottom right and the top left corners.

2. Draw a diagonal line connecting the two marks, extending the line to the edges of the fabric.

3. Repeat Steps 1 and 2 on the *right* side of a Fabric 2 rectangle, marking ½″ away from the bottom left and top right corners.

4. Position the rectangles right sides together with the Fabric 1 on top. Make sure that the diagonal lines align and pin in place. Sew a scant ¼″ seam on either side of the drawn line from Step 1. Using a ruler and rotary cutter, cut along the diagonal line to create two HRT units. Press the seams open.

5. Trim the HRT to the size specified in your project. Position an acrylic ruler so that the ¼″ intersection at the corner of the ruler aligns with the diagonal seam of the HRT (Fig. 2). The diagonal seam will not extend to the corner of the block because it is offset slightly. The seam will finish at the corner of the block.

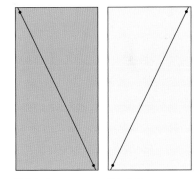

Fabric 1   Fabric 2

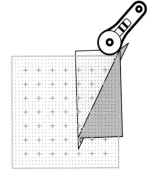

Figure 2

TIP When creating HRTs, it's important to use a scant ¼″ seam allowance. To do this, sew the seam slightly inside the ¼″ line. This produces more accurate angles when pressed.

PAPER PIECING BASICS

1. To make a template, draw a 6½″ square on a piece of 20 lb. paper and center a 6″ square inside that. From the lower left corner of the inner square, draw 4 lines using Figure 3 as a reference. Number each Section 1-5. (Fig. 3)

2. Cut fabrics a little bigger than you normally would for machine piecing. Beginning with Section 1, pin your fabric to the wrong side of the template, leaving at least ¼″ of fabric extending past the drawn lines. The right side of the fabric should be facing up. (Fig. 4)

3. After ensuring that your fabric selection for Section 2 also has at least ¼″ around all sides (hold the layers up to a sunny window to check), place the fabric for Section 2 on top of the fabric for Section 1, right sides together. Pin in place if needed. Flip over your template so that the numbers are facing you and the fabric is on the bottom.

4. Set your machine's stitch length to 1.8 mm. This will make removing the template paper a lot easier. Sew along the line between Sections 1 and 2, extending into the seam allowance.

5. Fold the paper along the sewn line so that the right sides of the paper are facing. Measure ¼″ away from the sewn line onto the exposed fabric. Trim away the excess fabric and press the seams to one side.

6. Repeat for all sections of the template, working in numerical order. (Fig. 5)

7. Press all seams again, this time on the right side of the fabric. (Fig. 6)

8. With the paper side facing up, trim around the template. Make sure to include any marked seam allowances. (Fig. 7)

BATTING

As a native Texan, I'm a big fan of 100% cotton batting as it's the perfect weight to snuggle under no matter the time of year. I especially love the wrinkles that are created after freshly laundering a completed quilt because the cotton quilt top, batting and backing both shrink but at a slightly different rate.

BASTING

Before basting a quilt sandwich, press the completed quilt top, backing and batting (if using a cotton batting) to remove any wrinkles. Because I like to use basting spray, I put together my quilts outside or in a well-ventilated area.

Position the quilt backing right side down on a large clean surface and secure the edges with painters tape. Next, center the quilt batting over the quilt backing, smoothing out the wrinkles. Fold back half of the batting towards the center of the quilt and spray the backing fabric with basting spray. Starting from the folded-over center, carefully unfold the batting back over the backing fabric, while smoothing out any wrinkles or bumps. Repeat this for the other side until the batting is entirely secured to the wrong side of the backing fabric.

Next, center the quilt top over the batting, right side up and repeat the spray basting process as you did for the backing and batting. If spray basting isn't your style, secure all three layers together using curved quilting safety pins or pin basting instead.

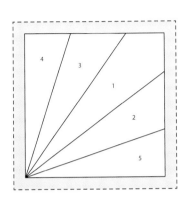

Figure 3

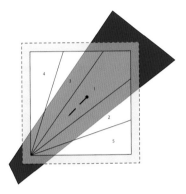

Figure 4

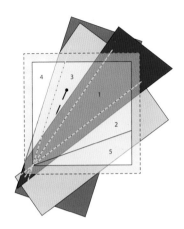

Figure 5

Figure 6

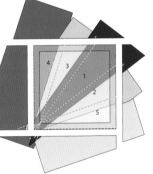

Figure 7

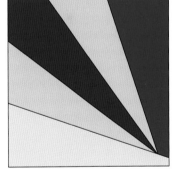

Completed Block

BINDING

Once your sandwich is completed and quilted, it's time to bind the quilt. If you've never created binding strips before, here is how I make them:

1. Based on the cutting instructions throughout the book, cut the total number of 2½″ × WOF strips indicated and trim the ends evenly.

2. With the right sides together, position one binding strip on top of and perpendicular to another binding strip, aligning the two adjacent edges. (Fig. 8)

3. Sew along the pressed line, creating a diagonal seam. Trim the excess fabric (Fig. 9), leaving a ¼″ seam allowance.

4. Press the seam open and trim the dog ears.

5. Repeat Steps 1-4 until all of the strips are joined.

6. Fold the binding strips in half, wrong sides together, along the length and press open. (Fig. 10)

7. Use your favorite binding technique to attach it to the quilt. I machine-bind on both the front and the back, but many quilters prefer to machine-bind on just the front and then hand-bind the back. Try both techniques until you find a method that works best for you.

TIP Before sewing binding strips together, fold over one short end of the strip, right sides together, forming a 45 degree angle. Press to form a crease at the angled fold. This establishes a clear sewing line to follow when joining your binding strips.

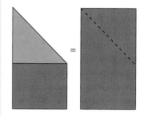

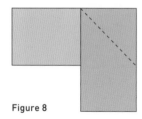

Figure 8

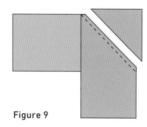

Figure 9

Figure 10

WASHING YOUR QUILT

Once a quilt is complete, I like to run it through the washer (cold water and delicate setting) and throw in six to eight Color Catchers, depending on the size of the quilt. Color Catchers are a quilter's best friend as they "catch" the excess dye from the fabric and eliminate any chance of the dye bleeding throughout the quilt. Depending on time I have available, I then place the quilt into the dryer or lay it out flat to dry on a hard surface.

West Texas

WIDE OPEN SPACES

1

Marathon

Marathon is located at the intersection of U.S. Highways 90 and 385, 26 miles southeast of the thriving metropolis of Alpine. Marathon is considered the gateway to Big Bend National Park. In September 1882, the estimated population was 130. As of the last census count, it was still only 470. This small town is home to big events like Marathon's annual Chili Cook-Off, 4th of July BBQ and dance, and the Viva Big Bend Music Festival.

My favorite places in Marathon ...

GAGE HOTEL
A beautiful historic hotel with lots of charm and only 45 minutes away from Big Bend.

V6 COFFEE BAR
Part of the Gage Hotel, V6 Coffee Bar is a charming café that serves breakfast and lunch.

FRENCH GROCER
Small grocery store with old-school charm and history. Excellent place to load up on provisions before heading to Big Bend.

WHITE BUFFALO BAR
Part of the Gage Hotel, the White Buffalo Bar is reputed to serve the best margaritas in town.

60½″ × 70½″

RUSTIC

MATERIALS

Fabric A: White, ¾ yard

Fabric B: Tan, 1⅓ yards

Fabric C: Orange, ⅝ yard

Fabric D: Red, 1 yard

Fabric E: Navy, 1⅓ yards

Backing Fabric: 4½ yards

Binding Fabric: ⅝ yard

Batting: 64″ × 74″

CUTTING

From Fabric A, cut:

   (6) 11″ squares for A1

   (2) 6″ squares for A2

From Fabric B, cut:

   (12) 11″ squares for B1

   (2) 6″ squares for B2

   (4) 5½″ squares for B3

From Fabric C, cut:

   (2) 11″ squares for C1

   (4) 6″ squares for C2

   (4) 5½″ squares for C3

From Fabric D, cut:

   (6) 11″ squares for D1

   (4) 6″ squares for D2

   (4) 5½″ squares for D3

From Fabric E, cut:

   (10) 11″ squares for E1

From the backing fabric, cut:

   (2) 81″ × WOF rectangles

From the binding fabric, cut:

   (7) 2½″ × WOF strips

The town of Marathon serves as the backdrop for the Gage Hotel. The hotel's website says, "For generations, the hotel has beckoned guests looking to escape the city frenzy, to relax and find inspiration in the stunning sunrises, sunsets and night skies." And that's just what I did. This quilt is all about that rustic scenery, the rich desert hues, miles and miles of unspoiled beautiful Texas landscape and some small-town vibes mixed in for good measure. If you go for a visit, be sure to grab a drink at the White Buffalo Bar. Cheers!

Quilted by Emily Bowers

Assembling the Half-Square Triangle (HST) Units

1. Referencing page 11, construct the following HST units. Press the seams open and trim each HST to 10½″ square.

(4) A1 + (4) E1= 8 HST squares

(6) E1 + (6) B1 = 12 HST squares

(2) A1 + (2) B1= 4 HST squares

(4) B1 + (4) D1= 8 HST squares

(2) D1 + (2) C1= 4 HST squares

2. Again referencing page 11, construct the following HST units. Press the seams open and trim each HST to 5½″ square.

(2) D2 + (2) C2 = 4 HST squares

(2) B2 + (2) D2 = 4 HST squares

(2) C2 + (2) A2 = 4 HST squares

TIP To minimize piecing mistakes, organize your fabric into HST groups based on the Assembly Diagram, before sewing.

Assembling the Quilt Top

1. Referencing the Assembly Diagram on page 25, arrange the plain squares and HST units into 8 rows.

2. Assemble Row 1 using (6) 5½″ HST units and (6) plain squares, paying attention to orientation. Repeat for Row 8. Press the seams open.

3. Assemble Row 2 using (6) 10½″ HST units, paying attention to orientation. Repeat for Rows 3–7. Press the seams open.

4. Stitch the rows together, being sure to match the seam lines. Press the seams open.

Finishing

1. Trim the two backing pieces along the selvage.

2. Position the backing pieces right sides together and sew along the long edge with a ½″ seam allowance. Press the seams open.

3. Reference the basting and binding instructions (see pages 12-14) and quilt as desired.

Share your progress, y'all

#rusticquilt

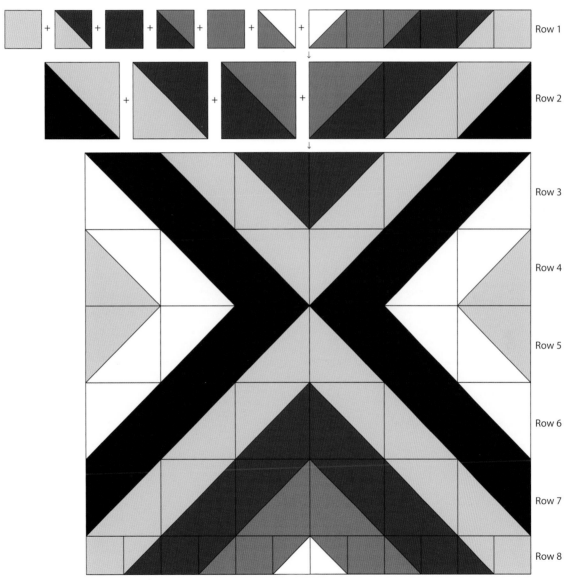

Row 1

Row 2

Row 3

Row 4

Row 5

Row 6

Row 7

Row 8

Assembly Diagram

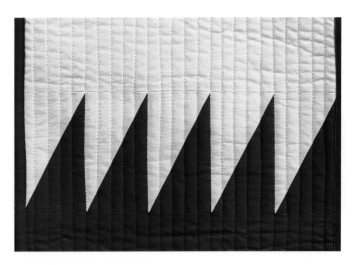

13″ × 28″

PORTALES MINI

MATERIALS

Fabric A: Putty, 1 fat quarter

Fabric B: Cream, 1 fat quarter

Fabric C: Burgundy, 1 fat quarter

Fabric D: Crimson, 1 fat quarter

Backing Fabric: ½ yard

Binding Fabric: ¼ yard

Batting: 17″ × 32″

CUTTING

From each of Fabrics A and D, cut:

   (1) 13″ × 3″ rectangle for A1 and D1

   (3) 5½″ × 3½″ rectangles for A2 and D2

From each of Fabrics B and C, cut:

   (1) 13″ × 5″ rectangle for B1 and C1

   (6) 5½″ × 3½″ rectangles for B2 and C2

From the binding fabric, cut:

   (3) 2½″ × WOF strips

Los Portales is part of the Gage Hotel and one of my favorite places to stay on the property. A cluster of twenty or so pueblo-style adobe brick rooms face a peaceful courtyard with flowers, trees, and a fountain. Each room is a little different, but they all have covered porches, authentic Saltillo tile floors, cowhide rugs, beautiful stone tile baths, and these amazing one-of-a-kind antique Mexican double doors. Those doors are what gave me the idea for this wall hanging.

Assembling the Half-Rectangle Triangle (HRT) Units

Referencing page 11, construct the following HRT units. Be sure to align the diagonal seam with the ¼" corners of the ruler, and mark the first rectangle listed from the bottom right to the top left (wrong side up) and the second rectangle from the bottom left to the top right (right side up). Press the seams open and trim each HRT to 5" × 3".

(3) A2 + (3) B2 = 6 HRT rectangles*

(3) B2 + (3) C2 = 6 HRT rectangles*

(3) C2 + (3) D2 = 6 HRT rectangles*

You will end up with one more HRT of each combination than you need.

Assembling the Quilt Top

1. Referencing the Assembly Diagram (adjacent), arrange the plain rectangles and HRT units into 7 rows.

2. Assemble Row 2 using 5 HRT units, paying attention to their orientation. Repeat for Rows 4 and 6. Press the seams open.

3. Stitch the rows together. Press the seams open.

Finishing

Reference the basting and binding instructions (see pages 12-14) and quilt as desired.

TIP Have fun! This mini comes together in no time so don't be afraid to raid your fat quarter stash and experiment with various colorways and prints.

Share your progress, y'all

#portalesminiquilt

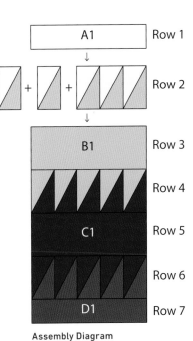

Assembly Diagram

Big Bend National Park

The Native Americans said that after making the Earth, the Great Spirit simply dumped all the leftover rocks on the Big Bend. It gets its name from the giant U-turn the Rio Grande makes in Southwest Texas. Covering 801,163 acres of West Texas, where the Chihuahuan Desert meets the Chisos Mountains, you'll find some of the prettiest hiking trails in the country.

My favorite places in Big Bend ...

CHISOS MOUNTAIN LODGE

Nestled in the Chisos Mountains, this rustic lodge is the only accommodation available in Big Bend National Park.

ROSS MAXWELL SCENIC DRIVE

Named after the park's first superintendent, this thirty-nine-mile drive starts near the western slopes of the Chisos Mountains and leads you to Santa Elena Canyon.

PANTHER JUNCTION VISITOR CENTER

Located near the center of the park, the visitor center is a great place to begin your visit and features a bookstore as well as an interactive exhibit of the park's mountain, river, and desert environments.

FOSSIL DISCOVERY EXHIBIT

Designed by famed Lake Flato Architects and located eight miles north of Panther Junction on the Persimmon Gap Entrance Road, the discovery center features the park's extensive collection of fossils.

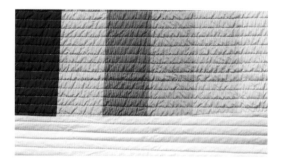

50½" × 60½"

MESA

MATERIALS

Fabric A: Deep Burgundy,
¼ yard

Fabric B: Brick Red, ¼ yard

Fabric C: Persimmon, ⅓ yard

Fabric D: Ochre, ⅓ yard

Fabric E: Coral, ½ yard

Fabric F: Peach, ⅓ yard

Fabric G: Almond, ⅓ yard

Fabric H: Natural, 1½ yards

Backing Fabric: 3¼ yards

Binding Fabric: ½ yard

Batting: 54" × 64"

CUTTING

From Fabric A, cut:

  (1) 4½" × WOF strip

    Subcut into:

    (1) 4½" × 16½" strip for A1

    (1) 4½" × 10½" strip for A2

From Fabric B, cut:

  (1) 6½" × 16½" strip for B1

From Fabric C, cut:

  (2) 4½" × WOF strips

    Subcut into:

    (1) 4½" × 24½" strip for C1

    (1) 4½" × 18½" strip for C2

From Fabric D, cut:

  (1) 4½" × 28½" strip for D1

  (1) 5½" × 22½" strip for D2

From Fabric E, cut:

  (3) 4½" × WOF strips

    Subcut into:

    (1) 4½" × 20½" strip for E1

    (1) 4½" × 14½" strip for E2

    (1) 4½" × 33½" strip for E3

    (1) 4½" × 26½" strip for E4

From Fabric F, cut:

  (1) 6½" × 37½" strip for F1

  (1) 4½" × 32½" strip for F2

From Fabric G, cut:

  (2) 6½" × 24½" strips for G1

  (1) 4½" × 32½" strip for G2

From Fabric H, cut lengthwise in
the following order:

  (2) 6½" × 50½" strips for H3

  (2) 6½" × 48½" strips for H2

  (1) 3½" × 32½" strip for H1

From the backing fabric, cut:

  (2) 58" × WOF rectangles

From the binding fabric, cut:

  (6) 2½" × WOF strips

There is a sense of calm that washes over me when I step out on the Lower Mesa Burro trail at Big Bend. I think it's the tranquility of being outdoors, the sunset hues, the desert vibes and the open skies that come together to make it one of my favorite places in Texas.

Quilted by Emily Bowers

Assembling the Quilt Top

1. The quilt is pieced using a similar construction method as the classic Log Cabin block. Position strips A1 and B1 right sides together and sew along the long side. Press the seam open.

2. Sew the A2 strip to the top edge of the unit from Step 1. Press the seam open.

3. Sew the E1 strip to the right edge of the unit from Step 2 (Fig. 1). Press the seam open.

4. Referencing the Assembly Diagram on page 37 for placement, continue adding the remaining strips. Press the seams open.

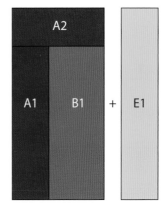

Figure 1

TIP When working with long strips, take the time to pin the strips together before sewing. This will ensure that the lengths stay aligned.

Finishing

1. Trim the two backing pieces along the selvage.

2. Position the backing pieces right sides together and sew along the long edge using a ½″ seam allowance. Press the seams open.

3. Reference the basting and binding instructions (see pages 12-14) and quilt as desired.

Share your progress, y'all

#mesaquilt

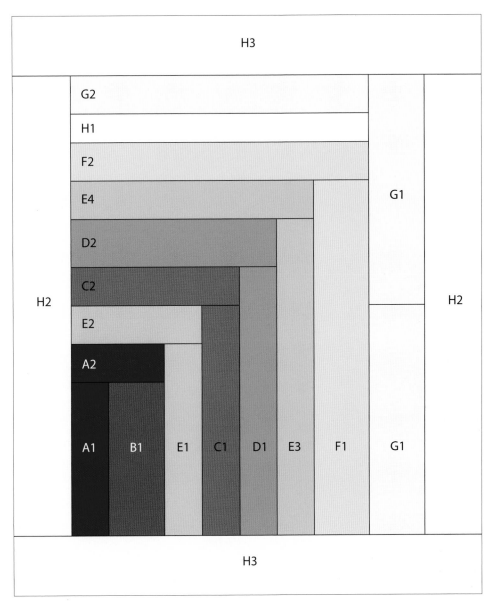

Assembly Diagram

64½″ × 76½″

CHIMNEY TRAIL

MATERIALS

Fabric A: Putty, ⅞ yard

Fabric B: Sand, ⅝ yard

Fabric C: Champagne, ⅝ yard

Fabric D: Tan, ⅞ yard

Fabric E: Natural, 3¼ yards

Backing Fabric: 4¾ yards

Binding Fabric: ⅔ yard

Batting: 68″ × 82″

CUTTING

From Fabric A, cut:

(1) 9″ square for A1

(2) 9″ × 17″ rectangles for A2

(2) 9″ × 17″ rectangles for A3

From Fabric B, cut:

(5) 9″ squares for B1

(1) 9″ × 17″ rectangle for B2

From Fabric C, cut:

(2) 9″ squares for C1

(2) 9″ × 17″ rectangles for C2

(1) 9″ × 17″ rectangle for C3

From Fabric D, cut:

(6) 9″ squares for D1

(1) 9″ × 17″ rectangle for D2

(1) 9″ × 17″ rectangle for D3

From Fabric E, cut lengthwise in the following order:

(2) 64½″ × 10½″ strips for E3

(14) 9″ squares for E1

(10) 9″ × 17″ rectangles for E2

From the backing fabric, cut:

(2) 85½″ × WOF rectangles

From the binding fabric, cut:

(8) 2½″ × WOF strips

I spotted the Chimneys while driving along the Ross Maxwell Scenic road through Big Bend National Park. I will never forget the way they looked alongside Kit Mountain—there was this warm glow, almost as if they were lit from the inside. I knew then it would be the perfect backdrop for this neutral-tone quilt.

Assembling the Half-Square Triangle Units

Referencing page 11, construct the following HST units. Press the seams open and trim each HST to 8½″ square.

(1) A1 + (1) E1 = 2 HST squares

(5) B1 + (5) E1 = 10 HST squares

(2) C1 + (2) E1 = 4 HST squares

(6) D1 + (6) E1= 12 HST squares

Assembling the Half-Rectangle Triangle Units

Again, referencing page 11 and the instructions below, construct the following HRT units. Be sure to align the diagonal seam with the ¼″ corners of the ruler. Press the seams open and trim each HRT to 16½″ × 8½″.

Mark the first rectangle listed from the bottom right to the top left (wrong side up) and the second rectangle from the bottom left to the top right (right side up).

(2) A3 + (2) E2 = 4 HRT rectangles*

(1) B2 + (1) E2 = 2 HRT rectangles*

(1) C3 + (1) E2 = 2 HRT rectangles

(1) D3 + (1) E2 = 2 HRT rectangles*

*You will end up with one more HRT of each combination than you need.

Mark the first rectangle listed from the bottom left to the top right (wrong side up) and the second rectangle from the bottom right to the top left (right side up).

(2) A2 + (2) E2 = 4 HRT rectangles*

(2) C2 + (2) E2 = 4 HRT rectangles*

(1) D2 + (1) E2 = 2 HRT rectangles*

*You will end up with one more HRT of each combination than you need.

NOTE Be sure to sew a scant ¼″ seam as the width of the pieced unit is 8½″ wide, before trimming. Take care not to use a larger seam allowance, or the HRTs will not be wide enough.

...there was this warm glow, almost as if they were lit from the inside.

Assembling the Quilt Top

1. Referencing the Assembly Diagram (opposite), arrange the HST units and HRT units into 7 rows of 6 blocks each.

2. Sew the blocks in each row together, paying attention to orientation. Press the seams open.

3. Stitch the rows together, being sure to match the seam lines. Press the seams open.

4. Sew the E3 borders to the top and bottom of the quilt top. Press the seams open.

Finishing

1. Trim the backing pieces along the selvage.

2. Position the two backing pieces right sides together and sew along the long edge using a ½″ seam allowance. Press the seams open.

3. Reference the basting and binding instructions (see pages 12-14) and quilt as desired.

Share your progress, y'all

#chimneytrailquilt

Quilted by Nancy Clement

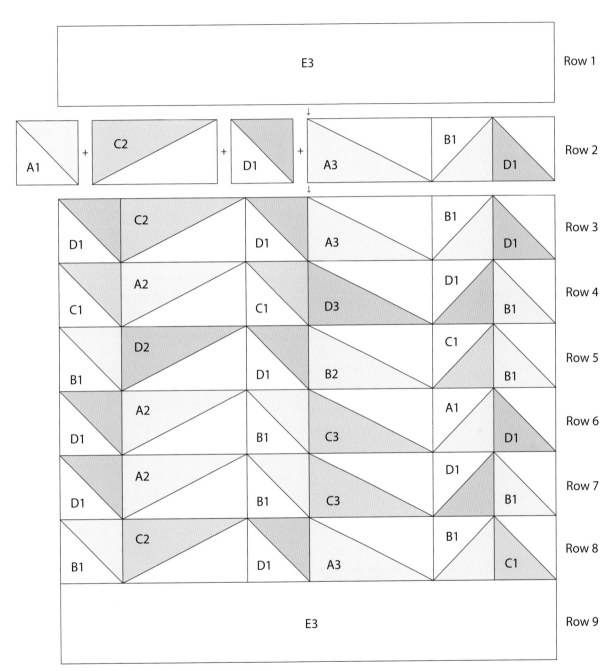

Assembly Diagram

Marfa

Marfa is a small desert town in West Texas at the junction of US Highways 90 and 67. It takes three hours to get there from the nearest major airport, which places it smack dab in the middle of nowhere. It was established in 1883, and for a long time its only claim to fame was as the film location for James Dean's final movie, *Giant.* Today, Marfa is a tourist destination and an arts hub. There is historical architecture, a classic Texas town square, modern art installments and plenty of art galleries and artisan shops. There is also a viewing platform just outside of town to kick back and watch the "Marfa Lights."

My favorite places in Marfa ...

CHINATI FOUNDATION
A gorgeous contemporary art museum based upon the ideas of its founder, Donald Judd. My favorite permanent installations include Judd's 100 untitled works in mill aluminum and Dan Flavin's large-scale colored fluorescent lights.

EL COSMICO
El Cosmico is a twenty-one acre nomadic hotel and campground. It is famous for its vintage trailers, safari and scout tents, Sioux-style tepees, and Mongolian yurts.

JETT'S GRILL
Grab a cocktail at Jett's Grill, part of the famed and historic Hotel Paisano, and relax outside in the beautiful courtyard while taking in the starry skies.

MARFA BOOK COMPANY
Located in the lobby of Hotel Saint George, the Marfa Book Company houses a unique selection of books and retail goods.

WRONG STORE
This art gallery owned by local artists Buck Johnson and Camp Bosworth is located in an old church off Main Street. Their gallery features the work of artists, including Camp, and unique objects carved out of reclaimed wood.

88½″ × 80½″

THUNDERBIRD

MATERIALS

Fabric A: Cream, 1⅝ yards

Fabric B: Cobalt, 5¼ yards

Backing Fabric: 8 yards

Binding Fabric: ¾ yard

Batting: 92″ × 84″

TIP Keep your pieces organized by labeling them with a sticky note as you work your way down the cutting chart.

CUTTING

From Fabric A, cut:

  (72) 4″ squares for A1

  (72) 3½″ squares for A2

From Fabric B, cut according to the Cutting Chart below:

  (72) 4″ squares for B1

  (8) 3½″ squares for B2

  (12) 3½″ × 6½″ rectangles for B3

  (8) 3½″ × 9½″ rectangles for B4

  (32) 3½″ × 10½″ rectangles for B5

  (4) 3½″ × 12½″ rectangles for B6

  (4) 3½″ × 18½″ rectangles for B7

  (2) 24½″ × 6½″ rectangles for B8

  (4) 16½″ × 6½″ rectangles for B9

  (2) 37½″ × 3½″ rectangles for B10

  (4) 37½″ × 9″ rectangles for B11

  (2) 3½″ × 7½″ rectangles for B12

  (4) 39″ × 7½″ rectangles for B13

From the backing fabric, cut:

  (3) 96″ × WOF rectangles

From the binding fabric, cut:

  (9) 2½″ × WOF strips

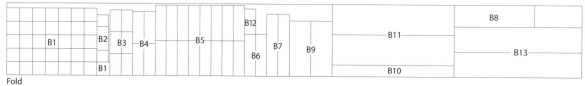

Selvages

Fold

Cutting Chart for Fabric B

The bright blue tile against the old Marfa National Bank building that faces the main street in Marfa, inspired the colors of the Thunderbird quilt. While a lot has changed in Marfa over the years, some things never do—such as the open skies that welcome you while strolling along the streets.

Quilted by Melissa Eubanks

Assembling the Half-Square Triangle Units

1. Referencing page 11, construct 144 HST units using the A1 + B1 squares.

2. Press the seams open and trim each HST to 3½″ square.

Assembling the Panels

The quilt is composed of two identical pieced panels, each with nine rows.

1. Arrange 72 assembled HST units, A2 plain squares and the B2-B9 rectangles into nine rows. (Fig. 1)

2. Beginning with Row 1, sew together the units paying careful attention to the HST orientation.

3. Repeat for the eight additional rows.

4. Sew the rows together to create the first panel and press the seams open.

5. Repeat Steps 1-4 for the second panel.

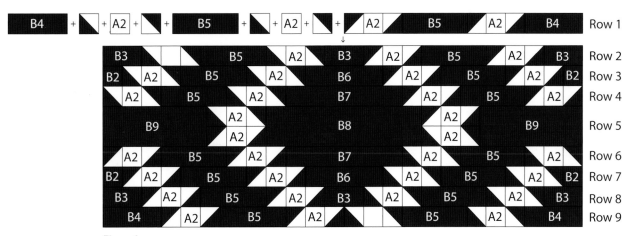

Figure 1

Assembling the Quilt Top

1. Position (2) B10 rectangles right sides together and sew along one short edge. Press the seam open.

2. Referencing the Assembly Diagram, join the two panels together with the B10 unit from Step 1.

3. Position (2) B11 rectangles right sides together and sew along a short edge. Press the seam open. Repeat to create two units.

4. Attach an assembled B11 unit to the top and to the bottom of the unit from Step 2 and set aside.

5. Attach a B13 rectangle to each long side of a B12 rectangle. Press the seams open. Repeat with the remaining B12 and B13 rectangles.

6. Attach a unit from Step 5 to either side of the assembled unit from Step 4 using the seams from the B12 rectangles to ensure perfect alignment with the B10 rectangles. Press the seams open.

Finishing

1. Trim the three backing pieces along the selvage.

2. Position two of the backing pieces right sides together and sew along the long edge using a ½″ seam allowance. Press the seam open.

3. Join the third backing piece and press the seam open.

4. Reference the basting and binding instructions (see pages 12-14) and quilt as desired.

Share your progress, y'all

#thunderbirdquilt

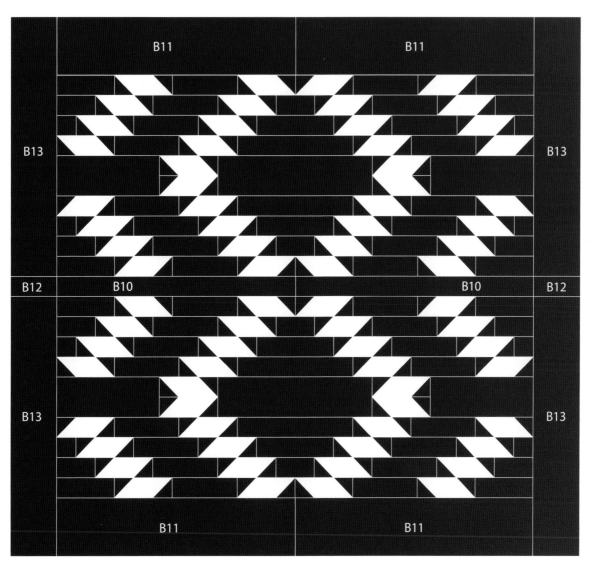

Assembly Diagram

60½″ × 64½″

MARFA LIGHTS

MATERIALS

Fabric A: Cream, ⅝ yard

Fabric B: Black, 3¾ yards

Backing Fabric: 4 yards

Binding: ⅝ yard

Batting: 64″ × 68″

CUTTING

From Fabric A, cut:

(7) 2½″ × WOF strips

Subcut in the following order* into:

(1) 2½″ × 28½″ strip for A8

(1) 2½″ × 14″ strip for A1

(1) 2½″ × 26½″ strip for A7

(1) 2½″ × 15½″ strip for A2

(1) 2½″ × 24½″ strip for A6

(1) 2½″ × 18½″ strip for A4

(1) 2½″ × 20½″ strip for A5

(6) 2½″ × 16½″ strips for A3

*cut in the order listed to minimize fabric wastage.

From Fabric B, cut:

(19) 2½″ × WOF strips

Subcut into:

(1) 2½″ × 2″ strip for B1

(1) 2½″ × 4½″ strip for B2

(1) 2½″ × 5½″ strip for B3

(2) 2½″ × 8½″ strips for B4

(1) 2½″ × 9½″ strip for B5

(4) 2½″ × 12½″ strips for B6

(2) 2½″ × 14½″ strips for B7

(2) 2½″ × 18½″ strips for B8

(1) 2½″ × 20½″ strip for B9

(1) 2½″ × 24½″ strip for B10

(2) 2½″ × 26½″ strips for B11

(2) 2½″ × 30½″ strips for B12

(3) 2½″ × 32½″ strips for B13

(2) 2½″ × 40½″ strips for B14

(4) 2½″ × 30½″ strips for B15

(8) 1½″ × WOF strips

Subcut into:

(8) 1½″ × 30½″ strips for B16

(8) 3½″ × WOF strips

Subcut into:

(8) 3½″ × 30½″ strips for B17

(2) 4½″ × WOF strips

Subcut into:

(2) 4½″ × 30½″ strips for B18

(4) 8½″ × WOF strips

Subcut into:

(4) 8½″ × 30½″ strips for B19

From the backing fabric, cut:

(2) 72″ × WOF rectangles

From the binding fabric, cut:

(7) 2½″ × WOF strips

This design is a nod to what is known as the "Marfa Lights." They are lights that seem to come from nowhere and dance on the horizon southeast of town (an area that is virtually uninhabited and extremely hard to get to). Some attribute them to natural phenomenon, some attribute them to paranormal activity. Whatever their source, the history of the Marfa Lights is intriguing and mysterious. The lights appear randomly throughout the night, a dozen or so nights a year, along the Mitchell Flat regardless of the season or weather.

Quilted by Melissa Eubanks

Assembling the Quilt Top

1. Referencing the Assembly Diagram (opposite), arrange the strips into 25 rows.

2. Beginning with Row 1, sew the strips in each row together. Press the seams open.

3. Pinning the rows to ensure proper alignment, sew the rows together. Press the seams open.

TIP To stay organized while piecing the rows, have a stack of sticky notes nearby and label each row (i.e. Row 1+2) as you piece them together.

Finishing

1. Trim the backing pieces along the selvage.

2. Position the two backing pieces right sides together, and sew along the long edge using a ½″ seam allowance. Press the seams open.

3. Reference the basting and binding instructions (see pages 14-15) and quilt as desired.

TIP To aid in the handling of the quilt top as it grows in size, consider sewing the rows together in pairs until two panels are formed, one of Rows 1-12 and the second as Rows 13-25. Then sew the final seam to attach the two halves.

Share your progress, y'all

#marfalightsquilt

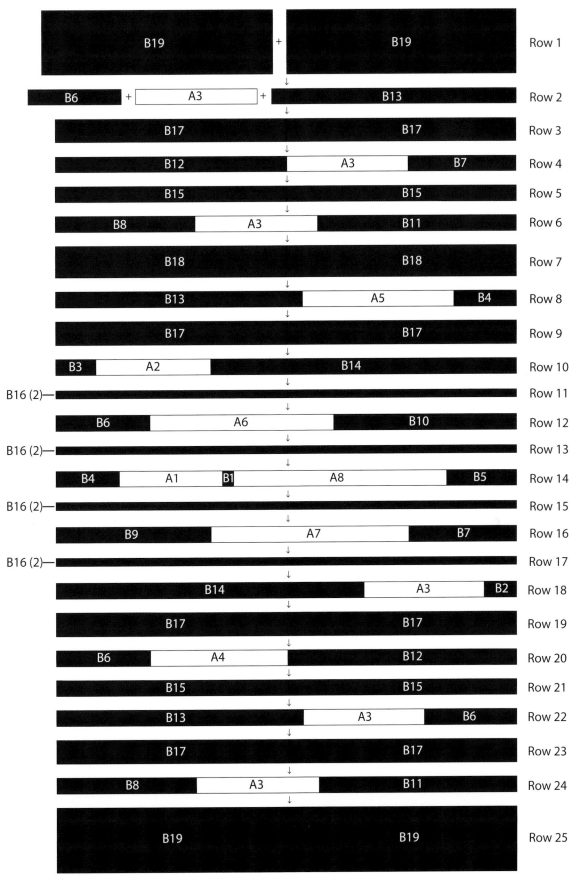

Assembly Diagram

59″ × 63½″

WANDERLUST

MATERIALS

Fabric A: Dark Gray, ⅝ yard

Fabric B: Medium Gray, ⅓ yard

Fabric C: Light Gray, ½ yard

Fabric D: Lightest Gray, ½ yard

Fabric E: White, ⅓ yard

Backing Fabric: 4 yards

Binding Fabric: ½ yard

Batting: 63″ × 67″

FOR THE PINK COLOR-WAY

Fabric F: Light Pink, ½ yard

Fabric G: Medium Pink, ⅓ yard

Fabric H: Dark Pink, ½ yard

Fabric I: Sangria, ⅔ yard

Fabric J: Bordeaux, ¾ yard

FOR THE BLUE COLOR-WAY

Fabric F: Gray-Blue, ½ yard

Fabric G: Medium Blue, ⅓ yard

Fabric H: Dark Blue, ½ yard

Fabric I: Navy, ⅔ yard

Fabric J: Darkest Blue, 1¼ yards

These quilts are an ode to El Cosmico—one of my favorite places to stay while in Marfa. I've never been to a place that was so vibrant and yet so serene at the same time. I will always remember the crystal clear view of the stars in the night sky and how big my friend Sara's eyes got when a rogue campfire spark almost caught her hair on fire. We laughed until we cried. Two color-ways have been created in honor of my favorite vintage trailers on the property—Vagabond (pink color-way) and Imperial Mansion (blue color-way).

Quilted by Emily Bowers

CUTTING

From Fabric A, cut:

  (2) 8″ × 29¾″ strips for A1

  (2) 2″ × WOF strips

    Subcut into:

    (1) 2″ × 42″ strip for A2

    (1) 2″ × 5″ strip for A3

From Fabric B, cut:

  (2) 3½″ × 29¾″ strips for B1

  (1) 2″ × WOF strip

    Subcut into:

    (2) 2″ × 13″ strips for B2

From Fabric C, cut:

  (2) 3½″ × 29¾″ strips for C1

  (3) 2″ × WOF strips

    Subcut into:

    (1) 2″ × 5″ strip for C2

    (1) 2″ × 42″ strip for C3

    (1) 2″ × 8½″ strip for C4

    (1) 2″ × 33″ strip for C5

From Fabric D, cut:

  (2) 5″ × 29¾″ strips for D1

  (2) 2″ × WOF strips

    Subcut in the following order into:

    (1) 2″ × 18½″ strip for D2

    (1) 2″ × 8½″ strip for D4

    (1) 2″ × 33″ strip for D3

From Fabric E, cut:

  (2) 3½″ × 29¾″ strips for E1

  (1) 2″ × WOF strip

    Subcut in the following order into:

    (1) 2″ × 18½″ strip for E2

    (1) 2″ × 13″ strip for E3

From Fabric F, cut:

  (2) 3½″ × 29¾″ strips for F1

  (3) 2″ × WOF strips

    Subcut in the following order into:

    (1) 2″ × 10″ strip for F2

    (1) 2″ × 5″ strip for F5

    (1) 2″ × 37″ strip for F3

    (1) 2″ × 42″ strip for F4

From Fabric G, cut:

  (2) 3½″ × 29¾″ strips for G1

  (1) 2″ × WOF strip

    Subcut into:

    (2) 2″ × 13″ strips for G2

From Fabric H, cut:

  (2) 3½″ × 29¾″ strips for H1

  (3) 2″ × WOF strips

    Subcut in the following order into:

    (1) 2″ × 5″ strip for H2

    (1) 2″ × 21½″ strip for H4

    (1) 2″ × 42″ strip for H3

    (1) 2″ × 20″ strip for H5

From Fabric I, cut:

  (2) 9½″ × 29¾″ strips for I1

  (1) 2″ × WOF strip

    Subcut into:

    (2) 2″ × 18½″ strips for I2

From Fabric J, cut:

  (2) 11″ × 29¾″ strips for J1

  (1) 2″ × WOF strip

    Subcut into:

    (1) 2″ × 11″ strip for J2

    (1) 2″ × 30½″ strip for J3

From the backing fabric, cut:

  (2) 72″ × WOF rectangles

From the binding fabric, cut:

  (7) 2½″ × WOF strips

TIP To stay organized while piecing the rows, have a stack of sticky notes nearby and label each row (i.e. Row 1+2) as you piece each row together.

Assembling the Quilt Top

1. Regardless which color-way you select, the labels on the Assembly Diagram are the same. Referencing the adjacent Assembly Diagram, arrange the strips into 19 rows.

2. Beginning with Row 1, sew the strips in each row together. Press the seams open. Repeat for the remaining 18 Rows.

3. Working with two rows at a time, sew together the rows into pairs and press.

4. Sew the assembled rows from Step 3 together until the quilt top is complete.

TIP When sewing long strips of fabric together, I like to set my seams while the fabrics are right sides together as I find this method nestles the stitches into the fabric and allows the seams to lay completely flat when pressed open. Set the seams with a spray of starch or starch alternative and using a dry hot iron, press the seams open. This method makes the strips more manageable by giving them a little added stiffness due to the starch too.

Finishing

1. Trim the two backing pieces along the selvage.

2. Position the backing pieces right sides together and sew along the long edge using a ½″ seam allowance. Press the seams open.

3. Reference the basting and binding instructions (see pages 12-14) and quilt as desired.

Share your progress, y'all

#wanderlustquilt

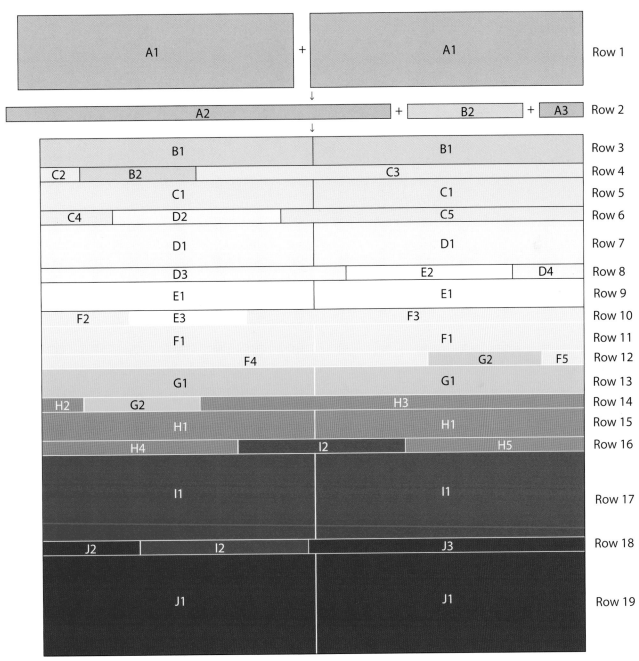

Assembly Diagram

2

New Mexico

THE LAND OF ENCHANTMENT

White Sands National Monument

Located 15 miles south of Alamogordo in southern New Mexico near the border of Texas, the White Sands National Monument was established by President Herbert Hoover in 1933. Standing amongst the dunes, taking in the blue skies and the distant mountain ranges, White Sands is breathtaking in person. It feels like another world as you hear the wind rustling the sand across the dunes. Visitors on a tight schedule are encouraged to call the day prior to arrival for information on road closures due to missile testing on the adjacent White Sands Missile Range. Please be sure to load up on plenty of water and sunscreen before entering the park.

My favorite places in White Sands ...

VISITOR CENTER

Before you start exploring, it's a good idea to stop by this great Visitor Center to get acquainted with the park and surrounding area.

INTERDUNE BOARDWALK

Located four-and-a-half miles from the Visitor Center, the raised boardwalk passes through the interdune area and ends at a gorgeous view point where you can view the Sacramento Mountains and dunefield landscape.

DUNES DRIVE

An eight-mile (13 km) scenic drive, Dunes Drive leads from the Visitor Center into the heart of the gypsum dunefield. This field of white sand dunes composed of gypsum crystals is the largest of its kind in the world.

SAND SLEDDING

If you're the adventurous type, I highly recommend sand sledding along the dunes near the Alkali Flat Trail. Sleds are available for purchase at the Visitor Center or you can bring your own.

SUNRISE PHOTOGRAPHY

Offered only twice a year and geared toward amateur and novice photographers. Join a ranger during the early morning hours to photograph the sunrise over the Sacramento Mountains.

48″ × 53″

MOSAIC

MATERIALS

Fabric A: White, 1¼ yards

Fabric B: Natural, 1¼ yards

Fabric C: Almond, 1 yard

Fabric D: Eggshell, 1⅝ yards

Fabric E: Tan, 1 yard

Backing Fabric: 3½ yards

Binding Fabric: ½ yard

Batting: 51″ × 56″

CUTTING

From Fabric A, cut:

   (35) 5½″ × 8½″ rectangles

From Fabric B, cut:

   (35) 4½″ × 9½″ rectangles

From each of Fabrics C and E, cut:

   (35) 5″ × 7″ rectangles

From Fabric D, cut:

   (35) 6″ × 9″ rectangles

From the backing fabric, cut:

   (2) 63″ × WOF rectangles

From the binding fabric, cut:

   (6) 2½″ × WOF strips

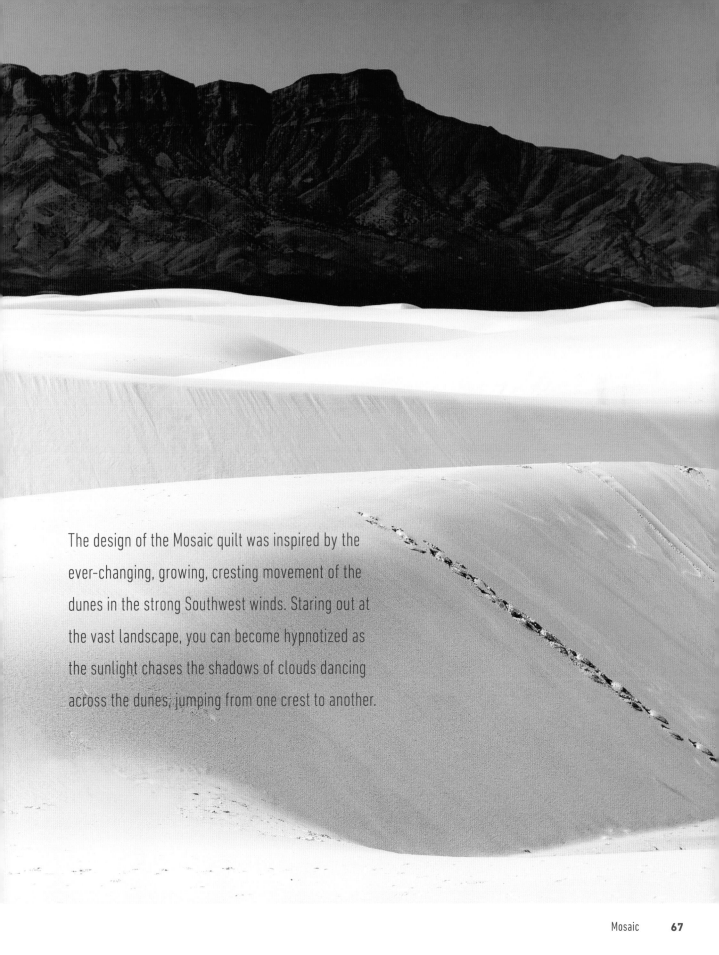

The design of the Mosaic quilt was inspired by the ever-changing, growing, cresting movement of the dunes in the strong Southwest winds. Staring out at the vast landscape, you can become hypnotized as the sunlight chases the shadows of clouds dancing across the dunes, jumping from one crest to another.

Quilted by Emily Bowers
Design inspiration credit by artist Angela Ferrrara

Assembling the Paper Pieced Blocks

1. Reference the Paper Piecing Basics on page 12 if necessary, then make 18 photocopies of Mosaic Templates 1 and 2 (see pages 134 and 135) and 17 photocopies of Mosaic Templates 3 and 4 (see pages 136 and 137). Copy templates at 125%.

2. Using Mosaic Template 1, paper piece a unit with an A1 rectangle in Area 1, a B1 rectangle in Area 2, and a C1 rectangle in Area 3. Leave the paper attached.

3. Using Mosaic Template 2, paper piece a unit with a D1 rectangle in Area 4 and an E1 rectangle in Area 5. Leave the paper attached.

4. Sew the two units together on the diagonal, right sides together, matching the corners and aligning the edges. Pin in place and stitch along the sew line (Fig. 1). Remove the paper in the seam allowance and press the seam to one side.

5. Repeat Steps 2–4 to create 18 paper pieced Block As and set aside.

6. Gather your photocopies of Mosaic Template 3 and Mosaic Template 4.

7. Using Mosaic Template 3, paper piece a unit with an A2 rectangle right side up in Area 1, a B2 rectangle in Area 2, and a C2 rectangle in Area 3. Leave the paper attached.

8. Using Mosaic Template 4, paper piece a unit with a D2 rectangle in Area 4 and an E2 rectangle in Area 5. Leave the paper attached.

9. Repeat Step 4 for Mosaic Templates 3 and 4.

10. Repeat Steps 7–9 to create 17 paper pieced Block Bs.

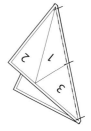

Figure 1

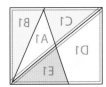

Block A: Make 18

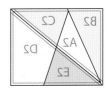

Block B: Make 17

Assembling the Quilt Top

NOTE Referencing Figure 2, note that some of the blocks are rotated 180 degrees. It is helpful to make stacks of blocks for each orientation and label them.

1. Referencing the Assembly Diagram opposite, arrange the blocks into 7 rows of 5 blocks each, paying attention to the orientation of the blocks.

2. Sew each row together. Remove the paper in the seam allowance for each row and press the seams to one side.

3. To complete the quilt top, sew the assembled rows together. Remove the paper and press the seams open.

Finishing

1. Trim the two backing pieces along the selvage.

2. Position the backing pieces right sides together and sew along the long edge using a ½˝ seam. Press the seams open.

3. Reference the basting and binding instructions (see pages 14-15) and quilt as desired.

Share your progress, y'all

#mosaicquilt

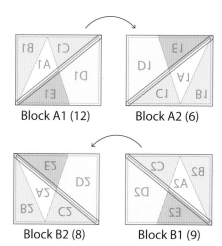

Block A1 (12)   Block A2 (6)

Block B2 (8)   Block B1 (9)

Figure 2

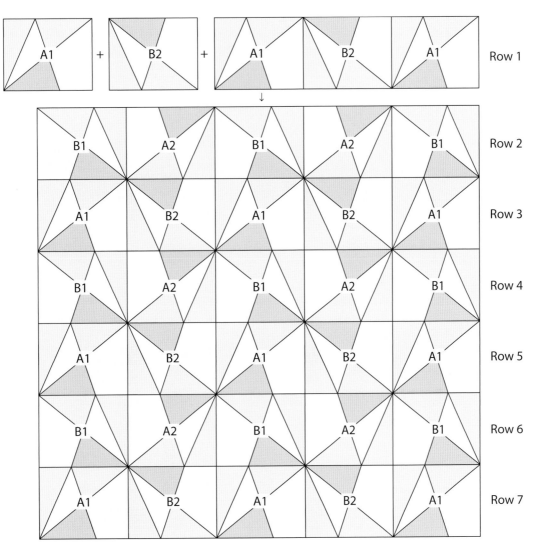

A1 + B2 + A1 B2 A1   Row 1

↓

B1 A2 B1 A2 B1   Row 2

A1 B2 A1 B2 A1   Row 3

B1 A2 B1 A2 B1   Row 4

A1 B2 A1 B2 A1   Row 5

B1 A2 B1 A2 B1   Row 6

A1 B2 A1 B2 A1   Row 7

Assembly Diagram

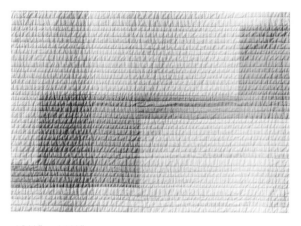

63½″ × 66½″

DUNES

MATERIALS

Fabric A: Oyster, ⅜ yard

Fabric B: Putty, ⅜ yard

Fabric C: Sand, ⅜ yard

Fabric D: Champagne, ⅜ yard

Fabric E: Tan, ¼ yard

Fabric F: White, 3 yards

Backing Fabric: 4 yards

Binding Fabric: ⅝ yard

Batting: 67″ × 70″

CUTTING

From Fabric A, cut:

(1) 2½″ × WOF strip

Subcut in the following
order into:

(1) 2½″ × 5″ rectangle for A1

(1) 2½″ × 14″ strip for A3

(1) 2½″ × 9½″ strip for A5

(1) 8½″ × WOF strip

Subcut in the following
order into:

(3) 5″ × 8½″ rectangles for A2

(1) 5″ × 6½″ rectangle for A4

From Fabric B, cut:

(1) 8½″ × WOF strip

Subcut into:

(4) 8½″ × 9½″ rectangles for B1

(1) 2½″ × WOF strip

Subcut into:

(3) 2½″ × 9½″ strips for B2

Inspired by the giant, wave-like dunes of Whites Sands, this pattern is intended to mimic how the gypsum sand moves across 275 square miles of desert. While walking along the dunes, you become mesmerized as the wind ripples the sand across the landscape. I find the serenity of the dunes, the wind and the open landscape both calming and inspiring.

Quilted by Nancy Clement

From Fabric C, cut:

(1) 8½″ × WOF strip

Subcut in the following order into:

(3) 8½″ × 9½″ rectangles for C3

(1) 5″ × 8½″ rectangle for C1

(1) 2½″ × WOF strip

Subcut into:

(7) 2½″ × 5″ rectangles for C2

From Fabric D, cut:

(1) 2½″ × WOF strip

Subcut into:

(4) 2½″ × 9½″ strips for D1

(1) 8½″ × WOF strip

Subcut into:

(3) 8½″ × 9½″ rectangles for D2

From Fabric E, cut:

(1) 5″ × WOF strip

Subcut into:

(3) 5″ × 6½″ rectangles for E1

(1) 2½″ × WOF strip

Subcut into:

(1) 2½″ × 14″ strip for E2

From Fabric F, cut according to the Cutting Diagram (below):

(10) 5″ × 6½″ rectangles for F1

(2) 5″ × 4½″ rectangles for F2

(2) 9½″ × 4½″ rectangles for F3

(4) 9½″ × 6½″ rectangles for F4

(8) 9½″ × 10½″ rectangles for F5

(1) 14″ × 6½″ rectangle for F6

(1) 14″ × 4½″ rectangle for F7

(2) 14″ × 10½″ rectangles for F8

(6) 18½″ × 10½″ rectangles for F9

(1) 5″ × 2½″ rectangle for F10

(1) 18½″ × 6½″ rectangle for F11

From the backing fabric, cut:

(2) 72″ × WOF rectangles

From the binding fabric, cut:

(7) 2½″ × WOF strips

Selvages

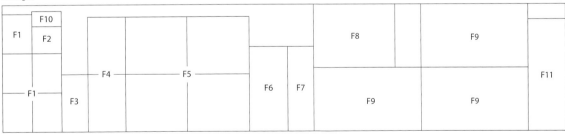

Fold

Cutting Diagram for Fabric F

Assembling the Quilt Top

1. Referencing the Assembly Diagram (opposite), arrange the A1–F11 blocks into 4 vertical columns.

2. Beginning with Column 1, assemble and piece together the cut units into blocks (indicated by the thicker lines on Columns 2-4 on the Assembly Diagram). Continue until all of the blocks are complete.

3. Sew the blocks together into 4 columns, paying close attention to placement.

4. Sew the 4 columns together to complete the quilt top. Press the seams open.

Finishing

1. Trim the backing pieces along the selvage.

2. Position the backing pieces right sides together and sew along the long edge using a ½" seam. Press the seams open.

3. Reference the basting and binding instructions (see pages 12-14) and quilt as desired.

Share your progress, y'all

#dunesquilt

Column 1   Column 2   Column 3   Column 4

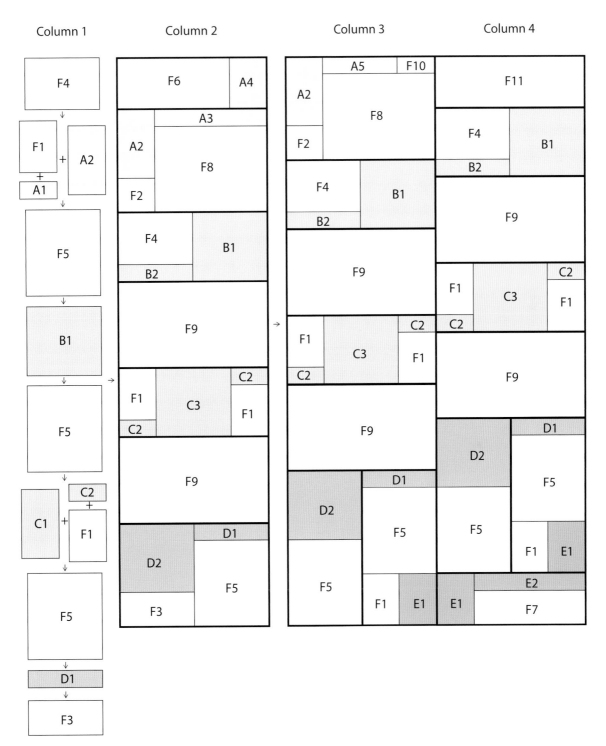

Assembly Diagram

Santa Fe

Santa Fe sits in the foothills the Sangre de Cristo Mountains in New Mexico. Founded by Spanish colonists in 1610, it is the oldest state capital city in the United States. It is known for its Pueblo-style architecture and crooked streets that wind past adobe landmarks. It is also a creative-arts hotbed—the New Mexico Museum of Art, Georgia O'Keefe Museum, Museum of Contemporary Native Arts, and more than 250 galleries call Santa Fe home.

My favorite places in Santa Fe ...

THE SHED
One of my go-to restaurants near the Santa Fe Plaza, the Shed never disappoints. For those of you who like spicy food, be sure to order the cheese enchiladas "Christmas style."

SHIPROCK SANTA FE
A beautiful gallery located on the Santa Fe Plaza, Shiprock Santa Fe carries jewelry, pottery, sculpture, basketry, folk art and fine art created by Native American artists. You'll find the most amazing collection of vintage Navajo textiles in the front room.

CANYON ROAD
Just east of the Santa Fe Plaza, Canyon Road is home to a slew of art galleries and is an art lover's paradise.

MUSEUM OF INTERNATIONAL FOLK ART
Located on Museum Hill, the museum houses a large collection of folk art, popular art, toys and textiles from around the world donated by the famous designer Alexander Girard and his wife.

SANTA FE OPERA
An open-air venue surrounded by the Sangre de Cristo and Jimenez mountain ranges, the Santa Fe Opera house plays host to a variety of operas each summer. Be sure to arrive extra early to enjoy and experience the fanciest tailgate party you've ever encountered.

49½″ × 63½″

SANDIA

MATERIALS

Fabric A: White, ⅓ yard

Fabric B: Sand, 2⅞ yards

Fabric C: Amber, ½ yard

Fabric D: Terracotta, 1 yard

Fabric E: Cinnamon, ½ yard

Fabric F: Brown, ¾ yard

Backing Fabric: 3¼ yards

Binding Fabric: ½ yard

Batting: 53″ × 67″

CUTTING

From Fabric A, cut:

(8) 4½″ × 9″ rectangles for A1

From Fabric B, cut:

(31) 8″ squares for B1

(22) 7½″ squares for B2

From Fabric C, cut:

(9) 4½″ × 9″ rectangles for C1

From Fabric D, cut:

(23) 4½″ × 9″ rectangles for D1

(3) 7½″ squares for D2

From Fabric E, cut:

(8) 4½″ × 9″ rectangles for E1

(4) 7½″ squares for E2

From Fabric F, cut:

(14) 4½″ × 9″ rectangles for F1

(3) 7½″ squares for F2

From the backing fabric, cut:

(2) 57″ × WOF rectangles

From the binding fabric, cut:

(6) 2½″ × WOF strips

For me, this one is all about taking a traditional quilt block and making it a bit more modern with the shape and color. It's an ode to the reddish colors of the Sandia Mountains at sunset—never the same, but always beautiful.

Quilted by Lee Jenkins

Assembling the Paper Pieced Blocks

1. Reference the Paper Piecing Basics on page 12 if necessary, then make 31 photocopies of the Sandia Template (see page 138). Copy at 100%.

2. Paper piece a Block A with a B1 rectangle in Area 1, a C1 rectangle in Area 2, and a D1 rectangle in Area 3. Leave the paper attached. Repeat to create a total of 9 Block As.

3. Paper piece a Block B with a B1 rectangle in Area 1, an A1 rectangle in Area 2, and an E1 rectangle in Area 3. Leave the paper attached. Repeat to create a total of 8 Block Bs.

4. Paper piece a Block C with a B1 rectangle in Area 1, a D1 rectangle in Area 2, and a F1 rectangle in Area 3. Leave the paper attached. Repeat to create a total of 14 Block Cs.

5. Trim Blocks A, B, and C to the edge of the paper piecing template, resulting in 7½″ square blocks.

Assembling the Quilt Top

1. Referencing the Assembly Diagram on page 85, arrange the paper-pieced blocks and the plain squares into 9 rows of 7 blocks each.

2. Sew each row together. Remove the paper in the seam allowance for each row and press the seams to one side.

3. To complete the quilt top, sew the assembled rows together, being sure to match up the seams. Remove the paper and press the seams open.

Block A: Make 9

Block B: Make 8

Block C: Make 14

Finishing

1. Trim the two backing pieces along the selvage.

2. Position the backing pieces right sides together and sew along the long edge using a ½″ seam allowance. Press the seams open.

3. Reference the basting and binding instructions (see pages 12–14) and quilt as desired.

Share your progress, y'all

#sandiaquilt

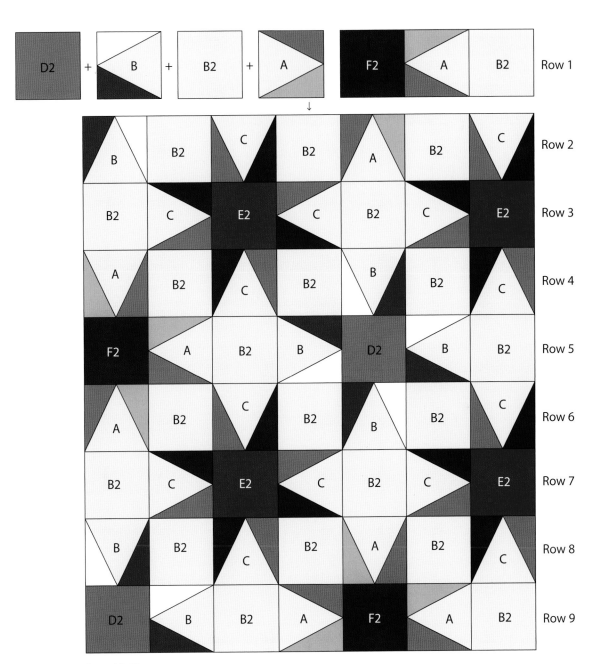

D2 + B + B2 + A   F2 A B2   Row 1

B   B2   C   B2   A   B2   C   Row 2

B2   C   E2   C   B2   C   E2   Row 3

A   B2   C   B2   B   B2   C   Row 4

F2   A   B2   B   D2   B   B2   Row 5

A   B2   C   B2   B   B2   C   Row 6

B2   C   E2   C   B2   C   E2   Row 7

B   B2   C   B2   A   B2   C   Row 8

D2   B   B2   A   F2   A   B2   Row 9

Assembly Diagram

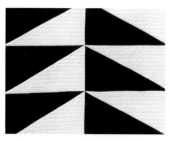 

75½″ × 70½″

ZUNI

MATERIALS

Fabric A: Black, 2⅛ yards

Fabric B: White, 3¾ yards

Backing Fabric: 4½ yards

Binding Fabric: ⅔ yard

Batting: 79″ × 74″

"ADOBE" ALTERNATE COLOR-WAY

Fabric A: Tomato Red, 2⅛ yards

Fabric B: Medium Red, 3¾ yards

CUTTING

From Fabric A, cut according to Cutting Diagram 1:

(16) 12½″ × 7″ rectangles for A1

(32) 8″ × 4″ rectangles for A2

From Fabric B, cut according to Cutting Diagram 2:

(16) 12½″ × 7″ rectangles for B1

(16) 7″ squares for B2

(2) 48½″ × 3½″ rectangles for B3

(2) 48½″ × 6″ strips for B4

(2) 75½″ × 11½″ rectangles for B5

From the backing fabric, cut:

(2) 81″ × WOF rectangles

From the binding fabric, cut:

(8) 2½″ × WOF strips

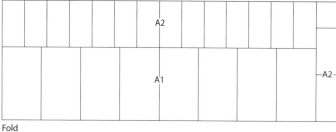

Cutting Diagram 1: Fabric A

Cutting Diagram 2: Fabric B

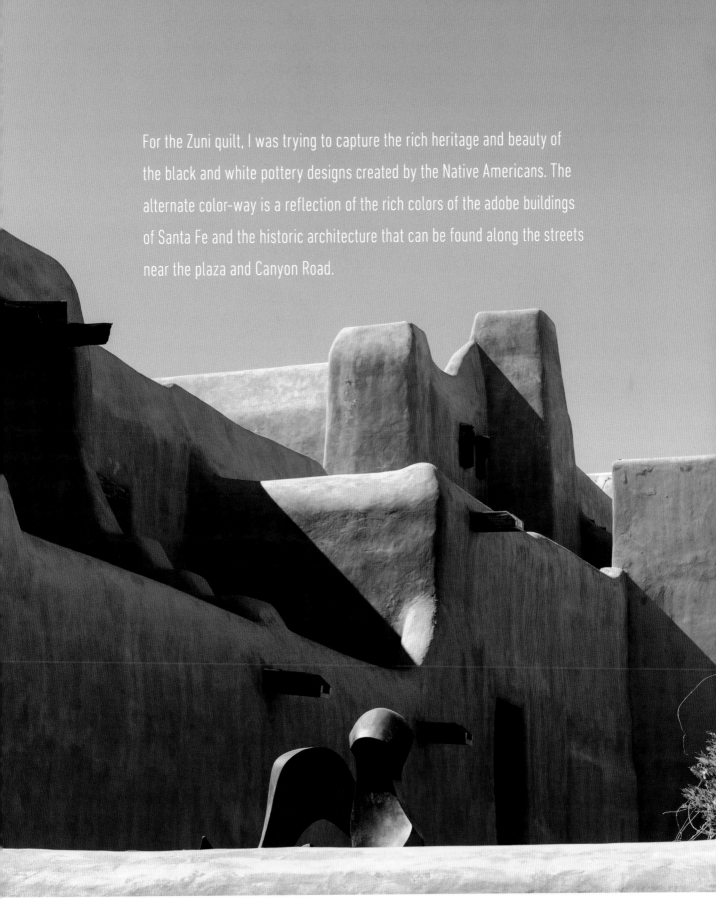

For the Zuni quilt, I was trying to capture the rich heritage and beauty of the black and white pottery designs created by the Native Americans. The alternate color-way is a reflection of the rich colors of the adobe buildings of Santa Fe and the historic architecture that can be found along the streets near the plaza and Canyon Road.

Quilted by Melissa Eubanks

Assembling the Half-Rectangle Triangles Units

1. Referencing page 11 and the instructions below, construct the following HRT units. Be sure to align the diagonal seam with the ¼″ corners of the ruler. Press the seams open and trim each HRT to 12″ × 6½″.

2. Mark the A1 rectangle from the bottom left to the top right (wrong side up) and the B1 rectangle from the bottom right to the top left (right side up).

Block A: (8) A1 + (8) B1 = 16 rectangles

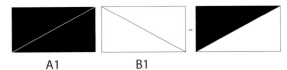

A1   B1

Block A: Make 16

3. Mark the A1 rectangle from the bottom right to the top left (wrong side up) and the B1 rectangle from the bottom left to the top right (right side up).

Block B: (8) A1 + (8) B1 = 16 rectangles

A1   B1

Block B: Make 16

Assembling the Paper Pieced Blocks

1. Reference the Paper Piecing Basics on page 12 if necessary, then make 16 photocopies of the Zuni Template (see page 139). Copy at 100%.

2. Paper piece a Zuni block with a B2 square in Area 1 and A2 rectangles in Areas 2 and 3 (Block C). Leave the paper attached.

3. Repeat Step 2 to create a total of 16 paper pieced Zuni blocks.

4. Trim the blocks to the edge of the paper piecing template, resulting in 6½″ square blocks.

TIP It's best to sew a scant ¼″ seam as the width of the pieced unit is 6½″ wide before trimming. Take care not to use a larger seam allowance, or the HRTs will not be wide enough.

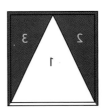

Block C: Make 16

Assembling the Quilt Top

1. Referencing the Assembly Diagram opposite, arrange the HRT blocks into 8 rows of 4 units each and the C blocks into two columns of eight blocks each.

2. Assemble each HRT row and press the seams open.

3. Sew the assembled HRT rows together, being sure to match up the seams.

4. Attach a B3 strip to the assembled unit from Step 3.

5. Attach an assembled column of C blocks to either side of the assembled unit from Step 4. Remove the paper from the C blocks and press the seams open.

6. Attach a B4 rectangle to either side of the assembled unit from Step 5 and press.

7. Attach a B5 rectangle to the top and bottom of the unit from Step 6 and press.

Finishing

1. Trim the backing pieces along the selvage.

2. Position the backing pieces right sides together and sew along the long edge using a ½″ seam allowance. Press the seams open.

3. Reference the basting and binding instructions (see pages 12-14) and quilt as desired.

Share your progress, y'all

#zuniquilt

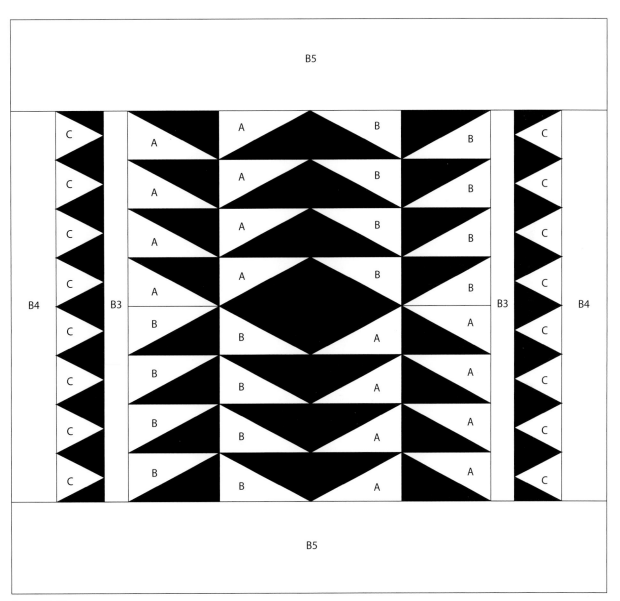

Assembly Diagram

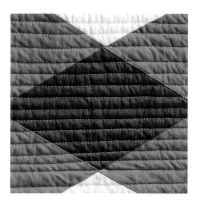

21″ × 43½″

ZIA MINI

MATERIALS

Fabric A: White, 1 yard

Fabric B: Aqua, ¼ yard

Fabric C: Medium Blue, ⅜ yard

Fabric D: Turquoise, ⅜ yard

Fabric E: Dark Blue, ¼ yard

Backing Fabric: 1½ yards

Binding Fabric: ⅓ yard

Batting: 25″ × 46″

CUTTING

From Fabric A, cut in the following order:

(2) 5½″ × 21″ rectangles for A3*

(2) 5½″ × 33½″ rectangles for A2*

(6) 4″ × 12″ rectangles for A1

*cut the fabric lengthwise

From Fabric B, cut:

(4) 6″ × 7½″ rectangles for B1

From Fabric C, cut:

(2) 4″ × 12″ rectangles for C1

(4) 6″ × 7½″ rectangles for C2

From Fabric D, cut:

(2) 4″ × 12″ rectangles for D1

(4) 6″ × 7½″ rectangles for D2

From Fabric E, cut:

(2) 4″ × 12″ rectangles for E1

From the binding fabric, cut:

(4) 2½″ × WOF strips

Growing up, my mom and I would peruse the Native American wares in front of the Palace of the Governors in the Santa Fe Historic District. It served as the seat of government for the state of New Mexico for centuries. I just remember all the beautiful turquoise jewelry created by the various Native American tribes. From the gorgeous turquoise colors to the detailed craftsmanship and elegant designs—the pieces were awe-inspiring.

Assembling the Paper Pieced Blocks

1. Reference the Paper Piecing Basics on page 12 if necessary, then make 6 photocopies of the Zia Templates (see pages 140 and 141). Copy at 125%.

2. Referencing Figure 1, paper piece two of each block using the following placement, leaving the paper attached.

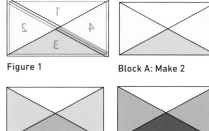

Figure 1   Block A: Make 2

Block B: Make 2   Block C: Make 2

BLOCK A

A1 rectangle in Area 1, B1 rectangles in Areas 2 and 4, and C1 rectangle in Area 3

BLOCK B

A1 rectangle in Area 1, C2 rectangles in Areas 2 and 4, and D1 rectangle in Area 3

BLOCK C

A1 rectangle in Area 1, D2 rectangles in Areas 2 and 4, and E1 rectangle in Area 3

3. Trim to the edge of the paper piecing template on all blocks, resulting in 6″ × 11″ blocks.

TIP When sewing together the two block sections, place a pin parallel between Areas 1 and 2 and push it through to the other side between Areas 3 and 4 to ensure the angles match.

Assembling the Quilt Top

1. Referencing the Assembly Diagram adjacent, arrange the 6 blocks vertically. Note that the second sets of blocks are flipped along the vertical to create a mirrored effect.

2. Sew together the blocks in the column. Remove the paper in the seam allowances and press the seams to one side.

3. Attach an A2 rectangle to either side of the unit from Step 2.

4. Attach an A3 rectangle to the top and bottom of the unit from Step 3. Remove the remaining paper and press the seams open.

Finishing

Reference the basting and binding instructions (see pages 12-14) and quilt as desired.

Share your progress, y'all

#ziamini

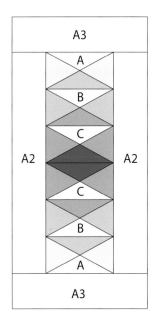

Assembly Diagram

64½″ × 70½″

CIELO

MATERIALS

Fabric A: White, 1¼ yards

Fabric B: Shadow, ⅜ yard

Fabric C: Slate Blue, ⅜ yard

Fabric D: Navy, 2½ yards

Backing Fabric: 4⅛ yards

Binding Fabric: ⅝ yard

Batting: 68″ × 78″

CUTTING

From Fabric A, cut:

   (7) 6″ squares for A1

   (2) 5½″ squares for A2

   (2) 12½″ × 35½″ rectangles for A3

From Fabric B, cut:

   (14) 6″ squares for B1

From Fabric C, cut:

   (14) 6″ squares for C1

From Fabric D, cut:

   (7) 6″ squares for D1

   (2) 5½″ × 30½″ rectangles for D2

   (2) 32½″ × 35½″ rectangles for D3

From the backing fabric, cut:

   (2) 73″ × WOF rectangles

From the binding fabric, cut:

   (7) 2½″ × WOF strips

Every summer, I get a sense of excitement and awe as I cross over the New Mexico state line. The design of this quilt portrays the subtle sense of wonder that can be found in the Land of Enchantment. For me, the large skies, low horizons, distant mountains, and voluminous clouds all come together in the Cielo quilt.

Quilted by Melissa Eubanks

Assembling the Half-Square Triangle Units

Referencing page 11, construct the following HST units. Press the seams open and trim each HST to 5½″ square.

(7) A1 + (7) B1 = 14 HST squares

(7) B1 + (7) C1 = 14 HST squares

(7) C1 + (7) D1 = 14 HST squares

Assembling the Quilt Top

1. Referencing Figure 1, arrange the A2 squares, the assembled HST units, and the D2 rectangles, paying close attention to the orientation of the HSTs.

2. For Rows 1–6, sew together the 3 HST units in each row and press the seams open. Sew the rows together, being sure to match the seams. Press the seams open and set aside.

3. Repeat Step 2 for Rows 9–14.

4. Assemble Rows 7 and 8, each composed of 3 HST units and one A2 square, and press the seams open. Sew the rows together, being sure to match the seams. Press and set aside.

5. Attach a D2 rectangle to the unit from Step 2.

6. Attach a D2 rectangle to the unit from Step 3.

7. Sew the unit from Step 5 to the top of the unit from Step 4 and press.

8. Sew the unit from Step 6 to the bottom of the unit from Step 7 and press.

9. Sew the (2) A3 rectangles together along one short edge and press the seams open. Attach the joined A3 rectangles to the left side of the unit from Step 8.

10. Sew the (2) D3 rectangles together along one short edge and press the seams open. Attach the joined D3 rectangles to the right side of the unit from Step 9, referencing the Assembly Diagram on page 99 for placement.

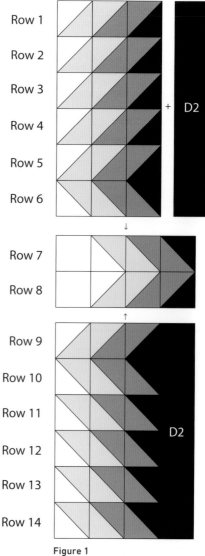

Row 1
Row 2
Row 3
Row 4
Row 5
Row 6
+ D2

Row 7
Row 8

Row 9
Row 10
Row 11
Row 12
Row 13
Row 14
D2

Figure 1

Finishing

1. Trim the two backing pieces along the selvage.

2. Position the backing pieces right sides together and sew along the long edge using a ½″ seam. Press the seams open.

3. Reference the basting and binding instructions (see pages 12-14) and quilt as desired.

Share your progress, y'all

#cieloquilt

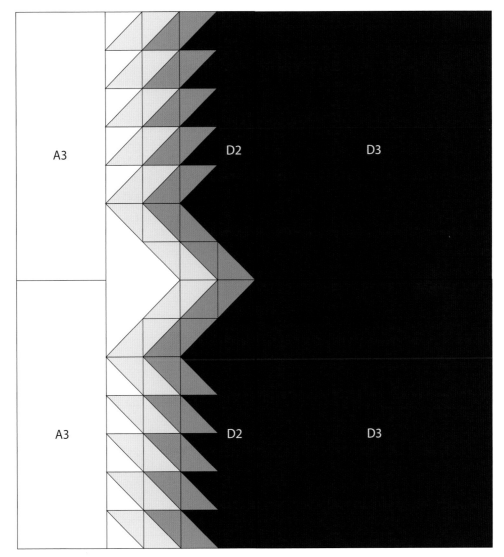

Assembly Diagram

Pecos National Historical Park

Pecos, specifically the National Historical Park, is known as the Gateway to the Plains. It's southeast of Santa Fe and home to what was once the largest Native American pueblo in the Southwest. More than 10,000 years of rich history surrounds this area, and it's where inspiration springs eternal for me. When visiting the park, be sure to check out the visitor center and watch the short film narrated by Greer Garson before venturing outside to the monument.

My favorite places in Pecos …

FRANKIE'S AT THE CASANOVA
You'll love the historic vibe while enjoying traditional New Mexican food in what was originally a general store built in 1910.

LISBOA SPRINGS TROUT HATCHERY
Built in 1921, this is the oldest fish hatchery in the state and is a fun place to visit with children as you can feed the fish.

60½″ × 70½″

KIVA

MATERIALS

Fabric A: Pale Pink, ¼ yard

Fabric B: Cantaloupe, ⅓ yard

Fabric C: Coral, ⅓ yard

Fabric D: Persimmon, ⅓ yard

Fabric E: Brick Red, ⅓ yard

Fabric F: Deep Burgundy, ¼ yard

Fabric G/Background: White, 2¼ yards

Backing Fabric: 3⅞ yards

Binding Fabric: ⅝ yard

Batting: 68″ × 78″

CUTTING

From each of Fabrics A and F, cut:

  (1) 5½″ × 30½″ rectangle for A1 and F1

  (1) 2″ × 36½″ strip for A2 and F2

From each of Fabrics B, C, D and E, cut:

  (1) 5½″ × 30½″ rectangle for B1, C1, D1 and E1

  (2) 2″ x 36½″ strips for B2, C2, D2 and E2

From Fabric G, cut according to the Cutting Diagram (below):

  (12) 3½″ × 5½″ rectangles for G1

  (5) 2″ × 36½″ strips for G2

  (2) 60½″ × 9¼″ strips for G3

  (2) 53″ × 12½″ rectangles for G4

From the backing fabric, cut:

  (2) 68″ × WOF rectangles

From the binding fabric, cut:

  (7) 2½″ × WOF strips

NEUTRAL ALTERNATE COLOR-WAY

Fabric A: Lightest Gray, ¼ yard

Fabric B: Light Gray, ⅓ yard

Fabric C: Medium Gray, ⅓ yard

Fabric D: Dark Gray, ⅓ yard

Fabric E: Darkest Gray, ⅓ yard

Fabric F: Black, ¼ yard

Cutting Diagram Fabric G

I spent many, many summers visiting the Pecos Historical National park with family and friends and each year I found the history of the monument humbling and inspiring. My favorite place to stop along the path to the monument is a restored Kiva, a subterranean pit that was used for religious and ceremonial purposes by the Pecos Native Americans, who believed the Kiva connected the spirits of the underworld with the world above. The colors and design of the Kiva quilts mimic the steps of the ladder, which leads you down to the circular, dark, cool adobe pit.

Quilted by Melissa Eubanks

Assembling the Quilt Top

1. Referencing Figure 1, sew two G1 rectangles to either side of the A1 rectangle and press the seams open. Set aside.

Figure 1

2. Repeat Step 1 with the B1, C1, D1, E1, and F1 rectangles and the remaining G1 rectangles.

3. Referencing Figure 2, sew G2, B2 and A2 together along their 36½″ side and press the seams open. Set aside.

G2
B2
A2

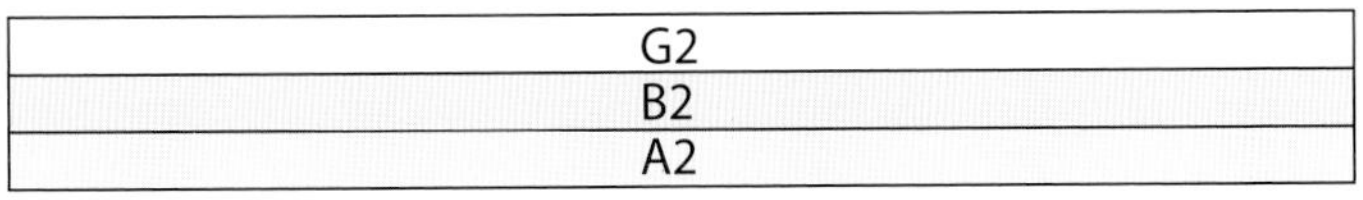

Figure 2

4. Repeat Step 3 with the remaining 2″ × 36½″ strips, referencing Figure 3 for placement.

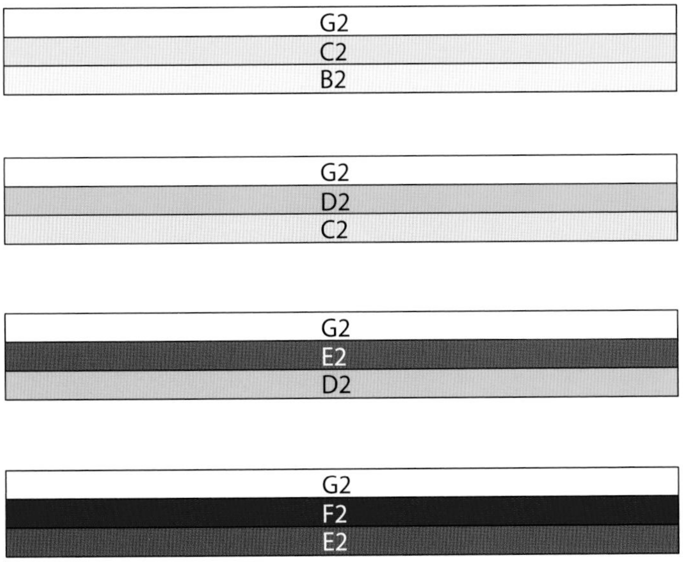

G2
C2
B2

G2
D2
C2

G2
E2
D2

G2
F2
E2

Figure 3

5. Referencing the Assembly Diagram (opposite), arrange the assembled units from Steps 1–4 and sew the rows together along the 36½″ sides. Press the seams open.

6. Sew a G4 rectangle to either side of the unit from Step 5. Press the seams open.

7. Sew a G3 rectangle to the top and bottom of the unit from Step 6. Press the seams open.

Finishing

1. Trim the two backing pieces along the selvage.

2. Position the backing pieces right sides together and sew along the long edge using a ½″ seam allowance. Press the seams open.

3. Reference the basting and binding instructions (see pages 12–14) and quilt as desired.

Share your progress, y'all

#kivaquilt

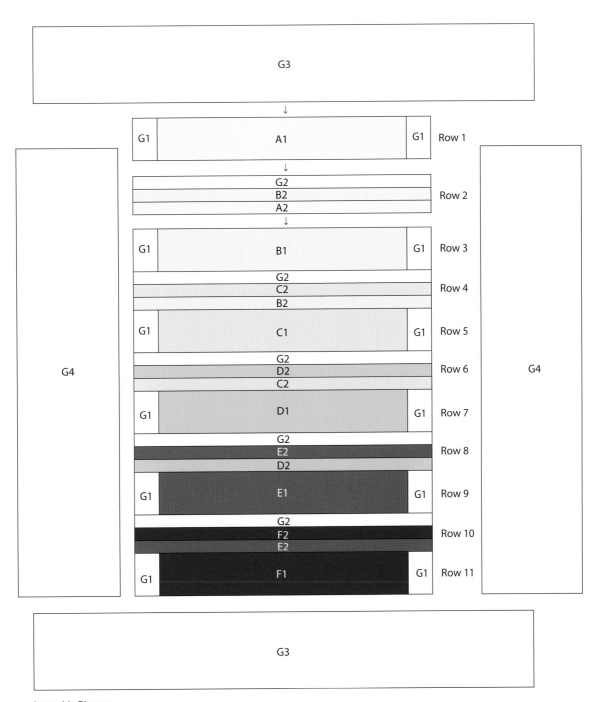

Assembly Diagram

Macho Canyon

Off the beaten path, in fact, completely cut off from civilization, there is a ranch nestled between two valleys, surrounded by a steep, narrow canyon of rocks and trees. This ranch has been in my family for generations. I spent summers here exploring the mountainside, hiking throughout the Santa Fe National Forest, discovering fossils, and listening to the wind rustle through the trees. My creativity flourishes while I'm here and this ranch is why I consider New Mexico to be my second home.

My favorite places near Macho Canyon ...

TERERRO GENERAL STORE
North of Macho Canyon, this family-owned and operated general store is the last stop for provisions for hikers and campers before entering the Pecos Wilderness.

JACK'S CREEK TRAIL
Near Tererro General Store, this nine-mile hike features fields of wildflowers and great views of the Pecos Wilderness peaks.

HAMILTON'S MESA TRAIL
Hamilton's Mesa Trail is my favorite hike and offers panoramic views of the Pecos Wilderness when you get to the top. Despite the very bumpy road to get to the trailhead, the view is well worth it once you arrive at Hamilton's Mesa.

HOLY GHOST CREEK TRAIL
Located east of Tererro, the trail is a moderate seven mile hike along the mountain stream with several switchbacks.

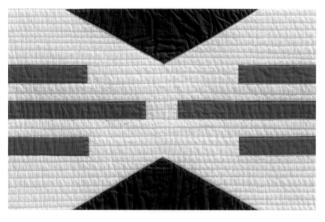

70½″ × 76¾″

ROSILLA PEAK

MATERIALS

Fabric A: Dark Navy, 1 yard

Fabric B: Turquoise, ¼ yard

Fabric C: White, 5 yards

Backing Fabric: 4¾ yards

Binding Fabric: ⅝ yard

Batting: 74″ × 81″

CUTTING

From Fabric A, cut:

    (30) 5″ × 8″ rectangles for A1

From Fabric B, cut:

    (4) 17¾″ × 1¾″ strips for B1

    (2) 26¼″ × 1¾″ strips for B2

From Fabric C, cut:

    (30) 5″ × 8″ rectangles for C1

    (6) 14½″ × 6½″ rectangles for C2

    (2) 8⅝″ × 6¾″ rectangles for C7

    (4) 14½″ × 26½″ rectangles for C8

    (4) 9½″ × 35½″ rectangles for C9

    (6) 1¾″ × WOF strips

        Subcut in the following order into:

        (1) 2¾″ × 1¾″ strip for C6

        (4) 4¾″ × 1¾″ strips for C3

        (2) 11¼″ × 1¾″ strips for C4

        (4) 27⅜″ × 1¾″ strips for C5

From the backing fabric, cut:

    (2) 85½″ × WOF rectangles

From the binding fabric, cut:

    (8) 2½″ × WOF strips

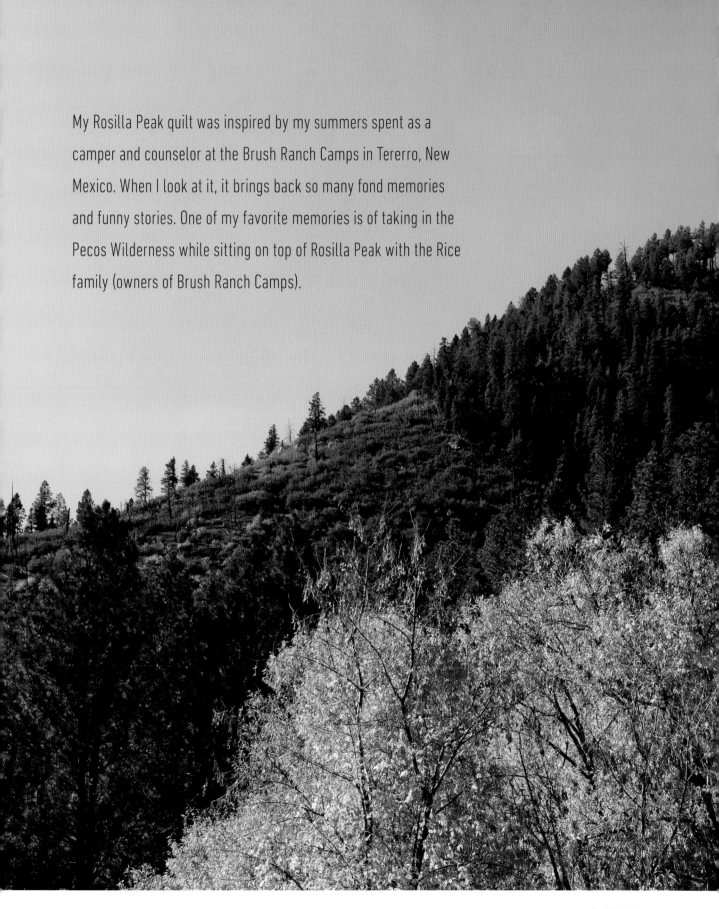

My Rosilla Peak quilt was inspired by my summers spent as a camper and counselor at the Brush Ranch Camps in Tererro, New Mexico. When I look at it, it brings back so many fond memories and funny stories. One of my favorite memories is of taking in the Pecos Wilderness while sitting on top of Rosilla Peak with the Rice family (owners of Brush Ranch Camps).

Quilted by Melissa Eubanks

Assembling the Half-Rectangle Triangle Units

1. Referencing page 11 and the instructions below, construct the following HRT units. Be sure to align the diagonal seam with the ¼″ corners of the ruler. Press the seams open and trim each HRT to 7½″ × 4½″.

2. Mark the first rectangle listed from the bottom left to the top right (wrong side up) and the second rectangle from the bottom right to the top left (right side up).

(15) A1 + (15) C1 = 30 HRT rectangles

3. Mark the first rectangle listed from the bottom right to the top left (wrong side up) and the second rectangle from the bottom left to the top right (right side up).

(15) A1 + (15) C1 = 30 HRT rectangles

Assembling the HRT Panels

1. Referencing Figure 1, join two HRTs together so that the Fabric As form a large triangle. Press the seams open. Repeat to create a total of 30 units.

2. Sew together 5 of the units from Step 1 into a column. Press the seams open. Repeat to create a total of six HRT columns.

3. Referencing Figure 2, attach a C2 rectangle to the end of an HRT column from Step 2, where the triangle points are facing. Press the seams open. Repeat to create a total of 4 units and set aside.

4. Repeat Step 3 with the remaining two HRT columns from Step 2, but place the C2 rectangle on the flat side of the triangle. Press the seams open.

5. Sew a unit from Step 3 to either side of a unit from Step 4 and press the seams open.

NOTE It's best to sew a scant ¼″ seam as the width of the pieced unit is 7½″ wide before trimming. Take care not to use a larger seam allowance, or the HRTs will not be wide enough.

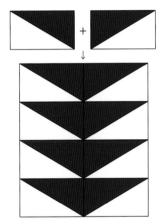

Figure 1

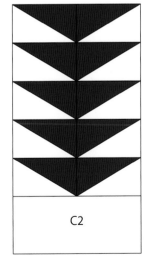

Figure 2

6. Sew a C8 rectangle to either side of each of the units from Step 5 (Fig. 3). Press the seams open and set aside. Repeat to create a total of 2 units.

Figure 3: Make 2

Assembling the Middle Strip Set

1. Referencing Figure 4, join the B1, C3, and C4 strips along the short edges to create a total of 2 strip units. Press the seams open and set aside.

2. Attach two C5 rectangles together along the short edges and press the seam open. Repeat to create a total of 2 strip units and set aside.

3. Attach a B2 strip to either side of a C6 strip along the short edges and press the seams open.

4. Attach a strip unit from Step 2 to the top and bottom of the strip unit from Step 3 along the long edges.

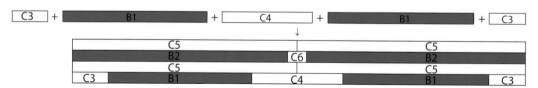

Figure 4

... one of my favorite memories is of taking in the Pecos Wilderness while sitting on top of Rosilla Peak

5. Attach a strip unit from Step 1 to the top and bottom of the strip unit from Step 4 along the long edges. Working slowly, press the seams in one direction, being careful not to introduce any shifting of the parallel strip sets.

6. Attach a C7 rectangle to either side of the strip unit from Step 5 along the short edges (Fig. 5). Press the seams open.

Figure 5

Assembling the Quilt Top

1. Sew an assembled HRT panel to the top and bottom of the assembled Middle Strip Set. Carefully press the seams open.

2. Attach two C9 rectangles together along the short edges and press the seam open. Repeat to create a total of two units.

3. Referencing the Assembly Diagram (opposite), sew a unit from Step 2 to the top and bottom of the assembled unit from Step 1. Carefully press the seams open.

Finishing

1. Trim the backing pieces along the selvage.

2. Position the two backing pieces right sides together and sew along the long edge using a ½″ seam allowance. Press the seams open.

3. Reference the basting and binding instructions (see pages 12-14) and quilt as desired.

Share your progress, y'all

#rosillapeakquilt

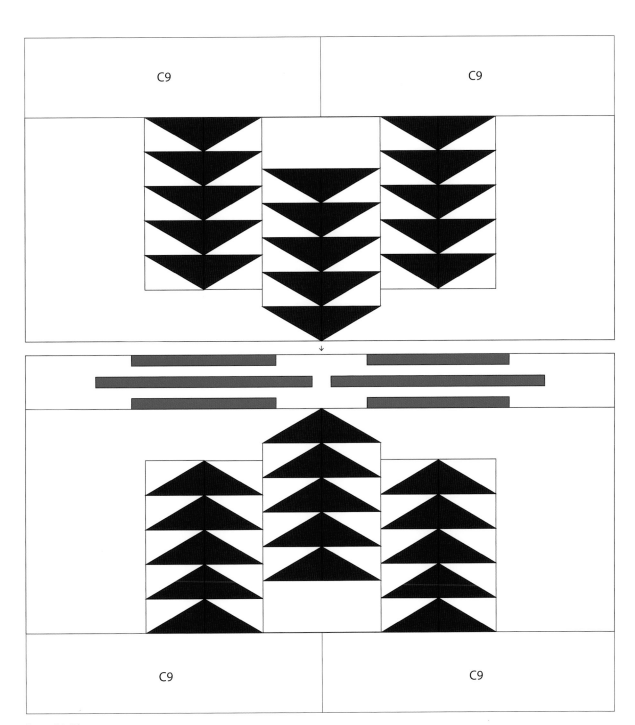

Assembly Diagram

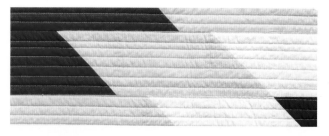

66½″ × 80½″

DALTON

MATERIALS

Fabric A: White, 1¾ yards

Fabric B: Deep Burgundy, ⅜ yard

Fabric C: Brick Red, 1⅜ yards

Fabric D: Almond, 2¾ yards

Backing Fabric: 5 yards

Binding Fabric: ⅝ yard

Batting: 70″ × 88″

CUTTING

From Fabric A, cut:

  (30) 5″ squares for A1

  (24) 4½″ squares for A2

  (12) 4½″ × 2½″ strips for A3

  (4) 12½″ × 4½″ strips for A4

  (8) 12½″ × 2½″ strips for A5

  (2) 2½″ × 6½″ strips for A6

From Fabric B, cut:

  (6) 5″ squares for B1

  (4) 4½″ squares for B2

  (4) 2½″ × 4½″ strips for B3

  (2) 2½″ × 12½″ strips for B4

  (2) 2½″ × 6½″ strips for B5

From Fabric C, cut:

  (24) 5″ squares for C1

  (20) 4½″ squares for C2

  (8) 2½″ × 4½″ strips for C3

  (4) 12½″ × 4½″ strips for C4

  (6) 12½″ × 2½″ strips for C5

TIP When working with pieces in various sizes and limited colors, I assign a unique sticky note color to each group and label every cut (e.g., A1, A2, A3, etc.) accordingly. This keeps the guesswork to a minimum when piecing.

From Fabric D, cut according to the Cutting Diagram below:

  (36) 5″ squares for D1

  (4) 2½″ × 4½″ strips for D2

  (4) 2½″ × 8½″ strips for D3

  (18) 4½″' × 6½″ rectangles for D4

  (8) 4½″ × 8½″ rectangles for D5

  (2) 4½″ × 12½″ strips for D6

  (10) 4½″ × 16½″ strips for D7

  (2) 4½″ × 24½″ strips for D8*

  (2) 4½″ × 32½″ strips for D9*

  * D8 and D9 are cut as full WOF strips

From the backing fabric, cut:

  (2) 90″ × WOF rectangles

From the binding fabric, cut:

  (8) 2½″ × WOF strips

Selvages

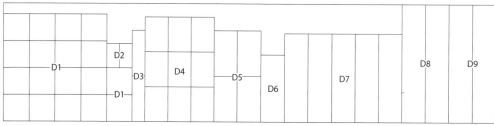

Fold

Cutting Diagram Fabric D

Dalton Canyon is a valley near Macho Canyon where you can see the Pecos River flowing by a colorful canyon rock backdrop. During the warmer months, you'll find numerous anglers fly-fishing for rainbow and brown trout along the river. As a child, I spent many summers there with friends and family, wading and splashing through the cold mountain stream. The design of this quilt is inspired by the log cabins along the Pecos River.

Quilted by Lee Jenkins

Assembling the Half-Square Triangle Units

1. Referencing page 11, construct the following HST units. Press the seams open and trim each HST to 4½″ square.

(18) A1 + (18) D1 = 36 HST squares

(6) A1 + (6) B1 = 12 HST squares

(6) A1 + (6) C1 = 12 HST squares

(18) C1 + (18) D1 = 36 HST squares

Assembling the Quilt Top

1. Referencing the Assembly Diagram (opposite) and using a flat surface or a design wall, arrange the HST units and the remaining plain pieces into 22 rows.

2. Beginning with Row 1, sew the units in each row together. Press the seams open.

3. After pinning the rows to ensure proper alignment, sew them together. Press the seams open.

TIP To aid in the handling of the quilt top as it grows in size, sew the rows together in smaller groups then join the groups to complete the quilt top.

Finishing

1. Trim the two backing pieces along the selvage.

2. Position the backing pieces right sides together and sew along the long edge using a ½″ seam allowance. Press the seams open.

3. Reference the basting and binding instructions (see pages 12-14) and quilt as desired.

Share your progress, y'all

#daltonquilt

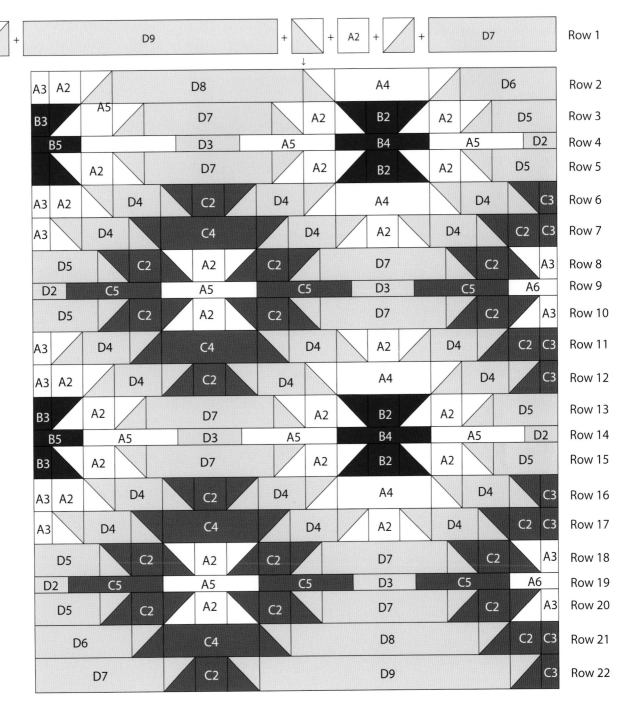

A3 + [triangle] + D9 + [triangle]↓ + A2 + [triangle] + D7 | Row 1

A3	A2	D8		A4	D6	Row 2
B3	A5	D7	A2	B2	A2	D5	Row 3
B5		D3	A5	B4	A5	D2	Row 4
	A2	D7	A2	B2	A2	D5	Row 5
A3	A2	D4	C2	D4	A4	D4	C3	Row 6
A3	D4	C4	D4	A2	D4	C2	C3	Row 7
D5	C2	A2	C2	D7	C2	A3	Row 8
D2	C5	A5	C5	D3	C5	A6	Row 9
D5	C2	A2	C2	D7	C2	A3	Row 10
A3	D4	C4	D4	A2	D4	C2	C3	Row 11
A3	A2	D4	C2	D4	A4	D4	C3	Row 12
B3	A2	D7	A2	B2	A2	D5	Row 13
B5	A5	D3	A5	B4	A5	D2	Row 14
B3	A2	D7	A2	B2	A2	D5	Row 15
A3	A2	D4	C2	D4	A4	D4	C3	Row 16
A3	D4	C4	D4	A2	D4	C2	C3	Row 17
D5	C2	A2	C2	D7	C2	A3	Row 18
D2	C5	A5	C5	D3	C5	A6	Row 19
D5	C2	A2	C2	D7	C2	A3	Row 20
D6	C4	D8	C2	C3	Row 21
D7	C2	D9	C3	Row 22

Assembly Diagram

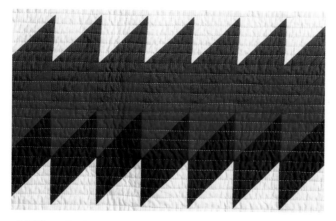

33½″ × 45½″

ANGELOS MINI

MATERIALS

Fabric A: Off-White, ½ yard

Fabric B: Natural, 1½ yards

Fabric C: Oatmeal, ¼ yard

Fabric D: Cocoa, ¼ yard

Fabric E: Earth, ⅛ yard

Fabric F: Brick Red, ⅛ yard

Fabric G: Dark Brown, ⅛ yard

Backing Fabric: 1½ yards

Binding Fabric: ½ yard

Batting: 37″ × 49″

CUTTING

From Fabric A, cut:

(40) 3½″ squares for A1

From Fabric B, cut lengthwise in the following order:

(2) 4½″ × 35½″ rectangles for B2

(2) 33½″ × 5½″ rectangles for B3

(30) 3½″ squares for B1

From each of Fabrics C and D, cut:

(20) 3½″ squares for C1 and D1

From each of Fabrics E, F, and G, cut:

(10) 3½″ squares for E1, F1, and G1

From the binding fabric, cut:

(5) 2½″ × WOF strips

Most of my quilts are inspired by places and things, but this one was inspired by a person. I grew up hearing family stories about the "crazy gold miner," Angelos, who lived up the canyon from our ranch. He would come down for dinner about once a month and would always bring his own food and drink (read: moonshine). A black-and-white photo of him resides in the bar where the photo was taken, along with family photos of my great grandfather who built the house in the late 1930's.

Assembling the Half-Square Triangle Units

1. Referencing page 11, construct the following HST units. Press the seams open and trim each HST to 3″ square.

(20) A1 + (20) B1 = 40 HST squares

(10) A1 + (10) C1 = 20 HST squares

(10) C1 + (10) D1 = 20 HST squares

(10) A1 + (10) D1 = 20 HST squares

(5) B1 + (5) E1 = 10 HST squares

(5) E1 + (5) F1 = 10 HST squares

(5) F1 + (5) G1 = 10 HST squares

(5) G1 + (5) B1 = 10 HST squares

Assembling the Quilt Top

1. Referencing the Assembly Diagram, arrange the HST units into 14 rows of 10 blocks each.

2. Sew the blocks in each row together and press the seams open.

3. Join the rows together along the long side and press the seams open.

4. Sew the B2 rectangles to either side of the unit from Step 3. Press the seams open.

5. Sew the B3 rectangles to the top and bottom of the unit from Step 4. Press the seams open.

Finishing

Reference the basting and binding instructions (see pages 12-14) and quilt as desired.

Share your progress, y'all

#angelosmini

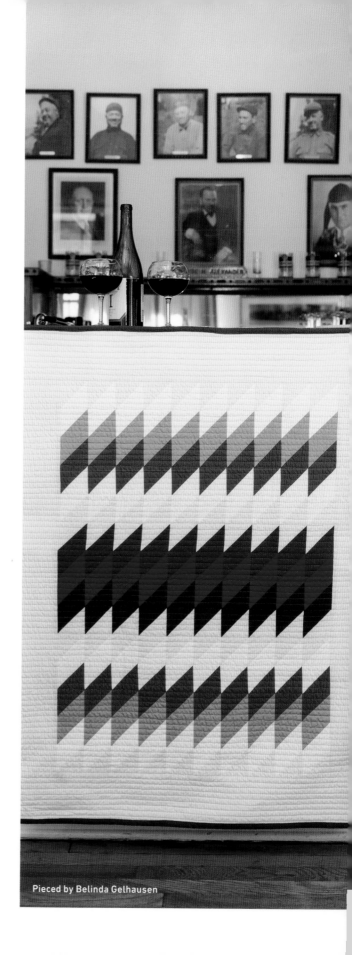

Pieced by Belinda Gelhausen

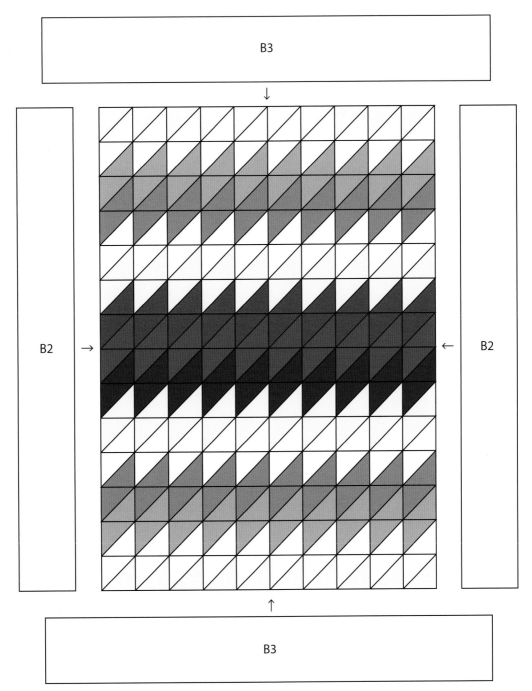

Assembly Diagram

72½″ × 80½″

MACHO CANYON

MATERIALS

Fabric A: White, 1⅛ yards

Fabric B: Navy, 1⅛ yards

Fabric C: Artichoke, 1¼ yards

Fabric D: Gray, 3 yards

Backing Fabric: 5 yards

Binding Fabric: ⅝ yard

Batting: 76″ × 84″

CUTTING

From each of Fabrics A and B, cut:

(48) 4″ × 7″ rectangles for A1
and B1

From Fabric C, cut:

(24) 4″ × 7″ rectangles for C1

(2) 6½″ × 36½″ rectangles for C2

From Fabric D, cut:

(24) 4″ × 7″ rectangles for D1

(4) 19½″ × 36½″ rectangles
for D2

From the backing fabric, cut:

(2) 90″ × WOF rectangles

From the binding fabric, cut:

(8) 2½″ × WOF strips

Our ranch has been in my family for generations. I've spent countless days enjoying the unique beauty of Macho Canyon. The design of this quilt was inspired by the rock canyon that faces the property, paired with the wide-open blue sky that sits above the forest skyline. Simply put: Mother Nature at its best, y'all.

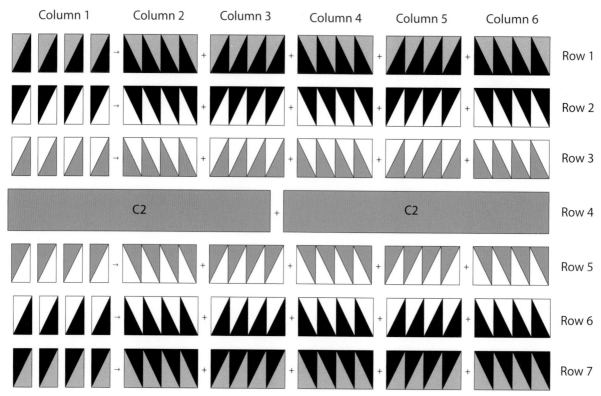

Figure 1

Assembling the Half-Rectangle Triangle Units

1. Referencing page 11 and the instructions below, construct the following HRT units. Be sure to align the diagonal seam with the ¼″ corners of the ruler. Press the seams open and trim each HRT to 6½″ × 3½″.

2. Mark the first rectangle listed below from the bottom left to the top right (wrong side up) and the second rectangle from the bottom right to the top left (right side up).

(12) A1 + (12) B1 = (24) HRT rectangles

(12) A1 + (12) C1 = (24) HRT rectangles

(12) D1 + (12) B1 = (24) HRT rectangles

3. Mark the first rectangle listed below from the bottom right to the top left (wrong side up) and the second rectangle from the bottom left to the top right (right side up).

(12) A1 + (12) B1 = (24) Reverse HRT rectangles

(12) C1 + (12) A1 = (24) Reverse HRT rectangles

(12) B1 + (12) D1 = (24) Reverse HRT rectangles

Assembling the Quilt Top

1. Sew the two Fabric C 6½″ × 36½″ rectangles together on the short side. Press the seam open.

2. Referencing Figure 1, Row 1 (opposite), arrange 24 assembled B1 + D1 HRT blocks in a row separated into six Columns, paying close attention to the orientation of the blocks.

3. Sew each set of four assembled HRT blocks together to form six Columns. Press the seams open and set aside.

4. Repeat Steps 2-3 for Rows 2, 3, 5, 6 and 7, using the HRT fabric combinations shown in Figure 1.

5. Arrange the assembled Rows from Steps 3 and 4 and the strip from Step 1 on a design wall or flat surface.

6. Sew the 7 Rows together and press.

NOTE It's best to sew a scant ¼″ seam as the width of the pieced unit is 3½″ before trimming. Take care not to use a larger seam allowance, or the HRTs will not be wide enough.

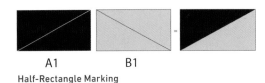

A1   B1

Half-Rectangle Marking

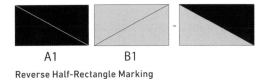

A1   B1

Reverse Half-Rectangle Marking

7. Sew two D2 rectangles together on their short side. Press the seams open. Repeat with the remaining two D2 rectangles.

8. Referencing the Assembly Diagram (opposite), attach an assembled unit from Step 7 to the top and bottom of the assembled unit from Step 6.

Finishing

1. Trim the backing pieces along the selvage.

2. Position the backing pieces right sides together and sew along the long edge using a ½″ seam allowance. Press the seams open.

3. Reference the basting and binding instructions (see pags 12-14) and quilt as desired.

Share your progress, y'all

#machocanyonquilt

Quilted by Lee Jenkins

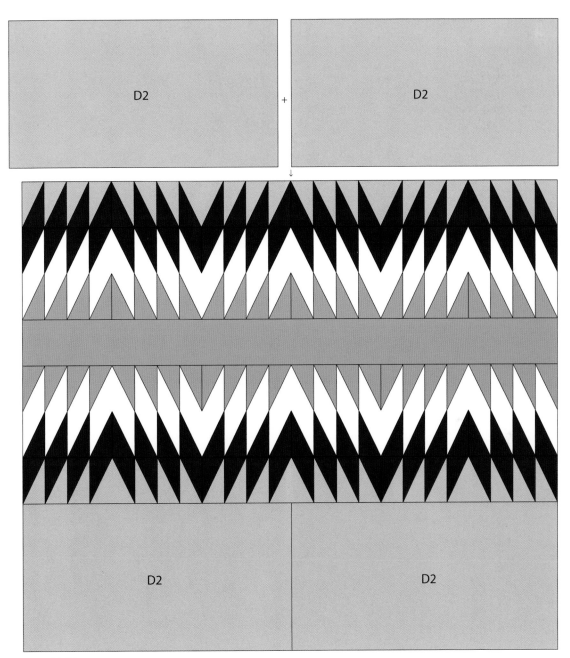

Assembly Diagram

Templates & Resources

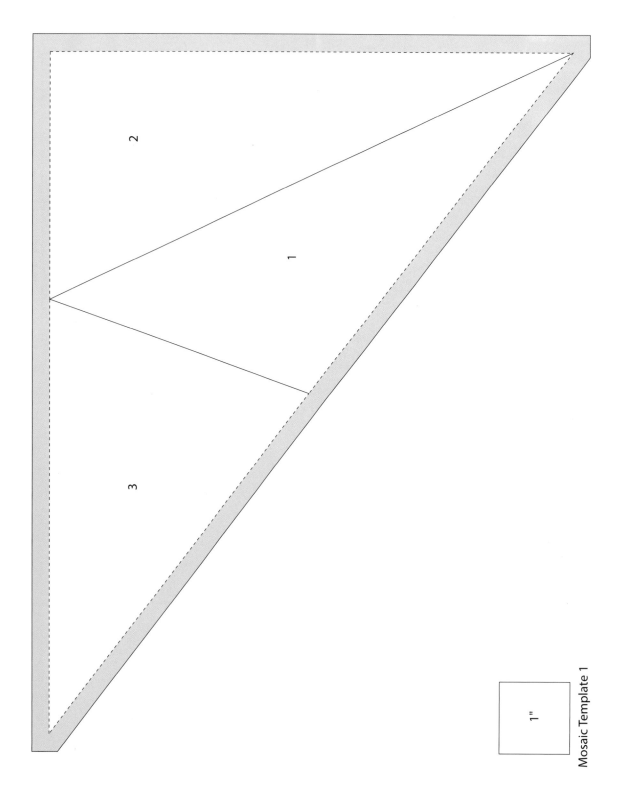

2

1

3

1"

Mosaic Template 1

MOSAIC TEMPLATES

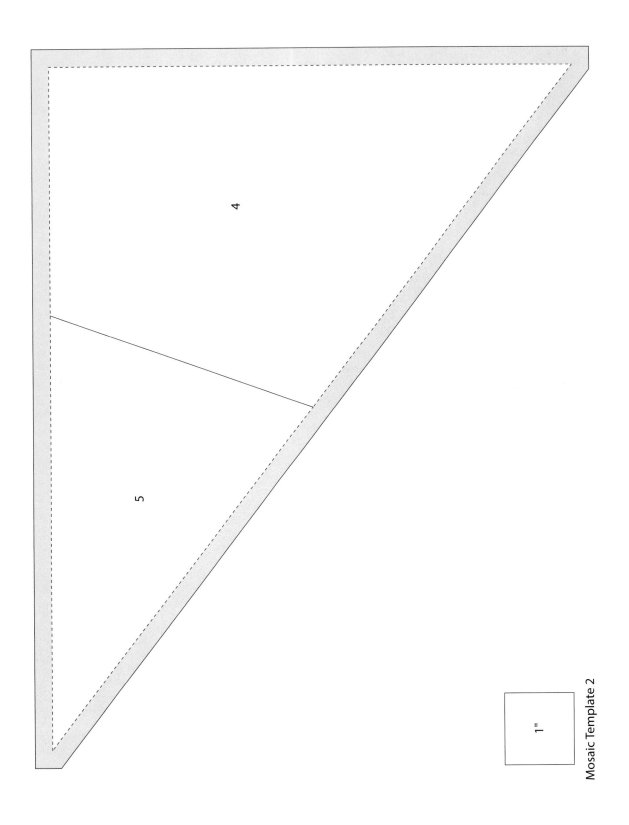

4

5

1"

Mosaic Template 2

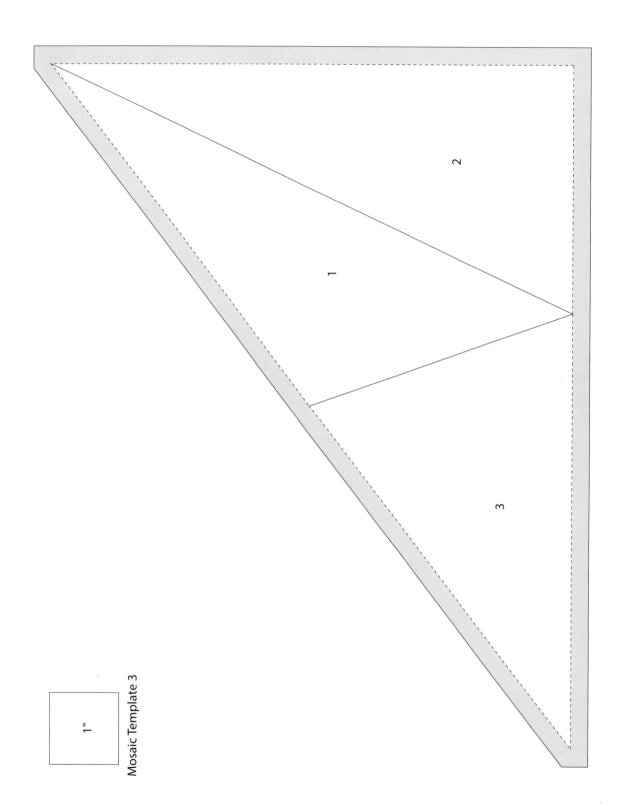

1"

Mosaic Template 3

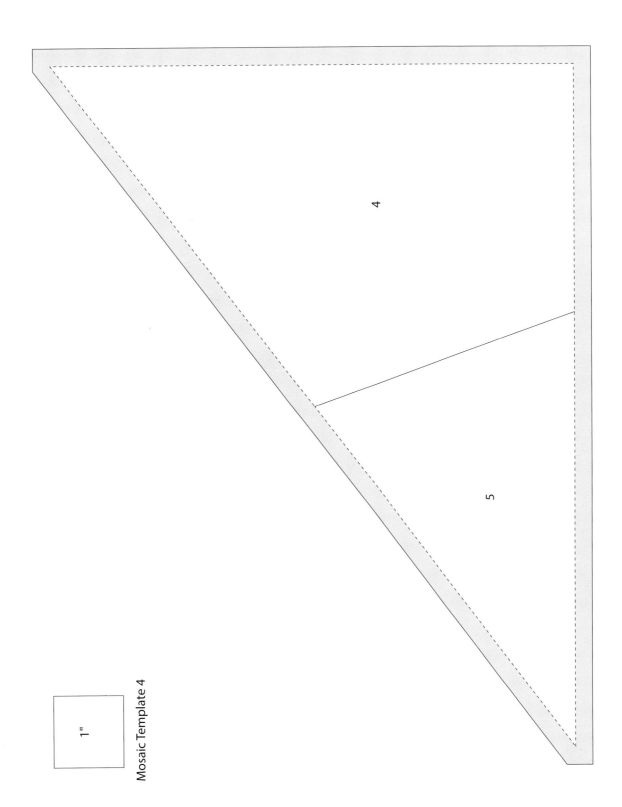

1"

Mosaic Template 4

4

5

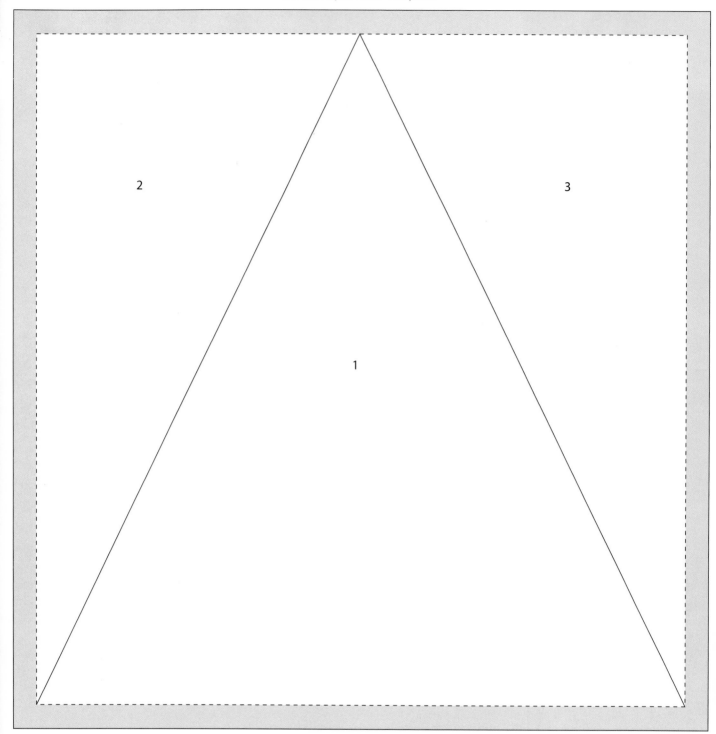

SANDIA
TEMPLATE

1"

Zuni Paper Piece Template

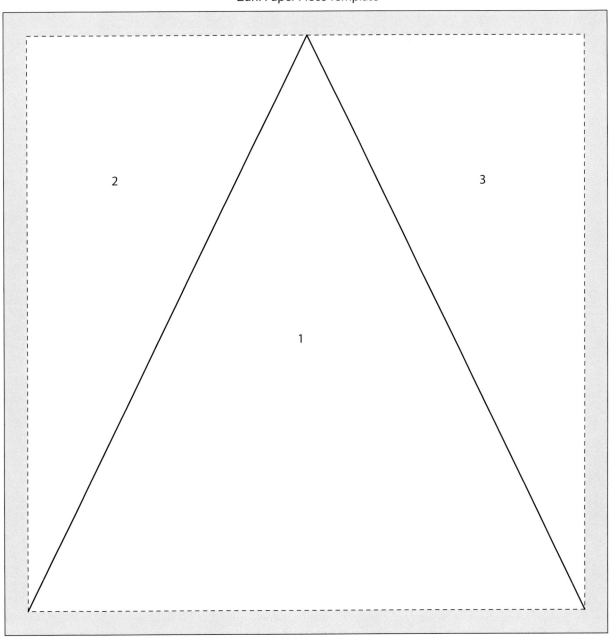

2

3

1

ZUNI
TEMPLATE

1"

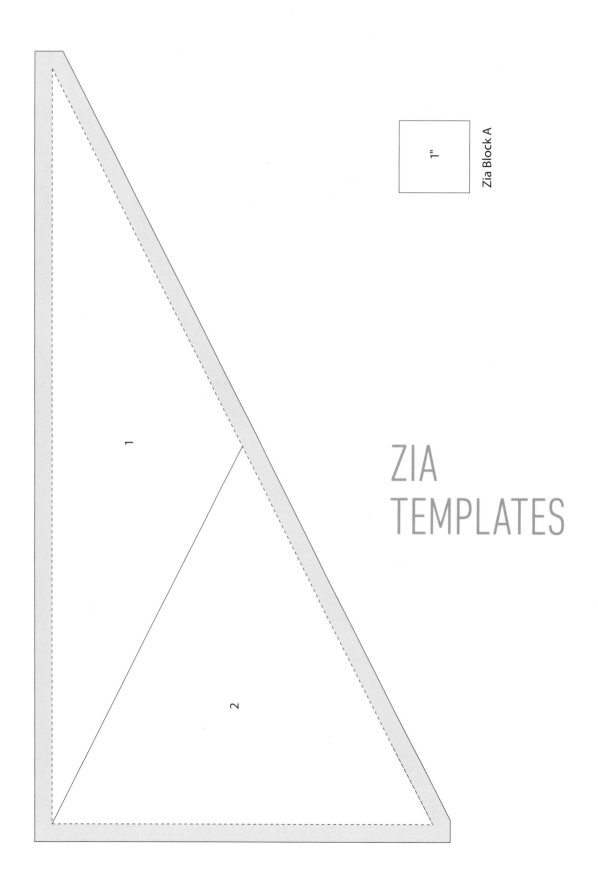

1

2

1"

Zia Block A

ZIA
TEMPLATES

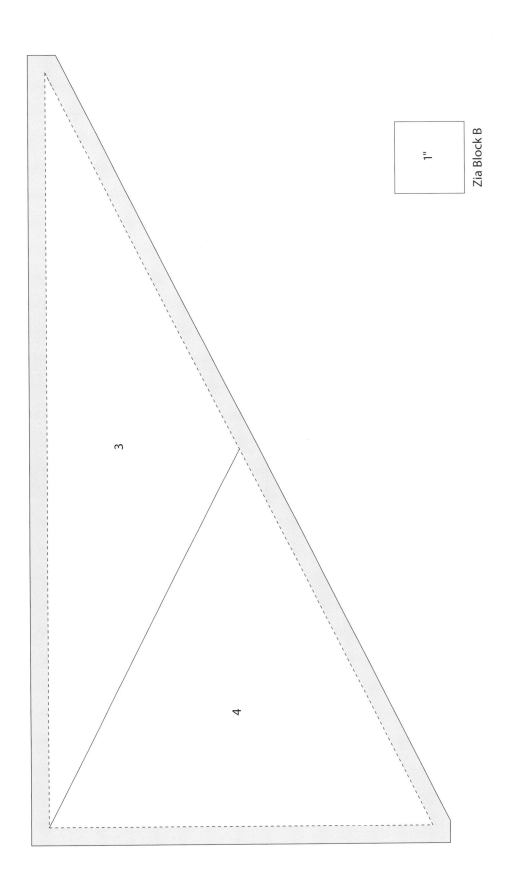

3

4

1"

Zia Block B

Resources

Below are some of my favorite sewing supplies and places you can find them.

Tools, Notions, and Accessories

AURIFIL THREADS

www.aurifil.com

50-weight thread for machine piecing and quilting

DRITZ

www.dritz.com

Curved safety pins and flat flower head pins

KAI

www.kaiscissors.com

Kai scissors 7000 series

MARY ELLEN PRODUCTS

www.maryellenproducts.com

Mary Ellen's Best Press starch alternative

NANCY'S NOTIONS

www.nancysnotions.com

Original Big Board (ironing board top)

ODIF

www.odifusa.com

505 Spray and Fix adhesive

OLFA

www.olfa.com

Rotary cutters and self-healing cutting mats

OMNIGRID

www.omnigrid.com

Rulers

ROWENTA

www.rowentausa.com

Iron

SHOUT COLOR CATCHER

www.shoutitout.com

Color catchers

Fabric

ME+YOU FABRICS

www.meandyoufabrics.com

Indah batiks and solids

MODA

www.unitednotions.com

Bella solids

ROBERT KAUFMAN FABRICS

www.robertkaufman.com

Kona cotton solids

Acknowledgments

To my dearest friends and family — Mom, Dad, Grandma, Dean, Lila, Holland, Hemi, Jen, Sara, Stephanie, Julie, Tiffany, Shandi, Belinda, Chris, and Darren — thank you so much for all of your love, laughter, and continuous support this past year.

Sincerest thanks to my editor, Susanne, and the talented team of people at Lucky Spool for allowing me to turn my crazy travel idea into a reality. Your advice and expertise means the world to me.

A special thank-you to Robert Kaufman, Moda, and Me+You Fabrics for generously providing all of the fabric used in the book. The solids were a dream to work with.

Big thanks to the fabulous and extremely talented photographer Kurt Griesbach. It was an absolute joy to work with you again, and I'm so proud of what we have created together.

Last but certainly not least, a huge thanks goes out to my very talented group of long-arm quilters — Emily Bowers, Nancy Clement, Melissa Eubanks, and Lee Jenkins. The quilts featured in this book would not have happened without you. Thank you!

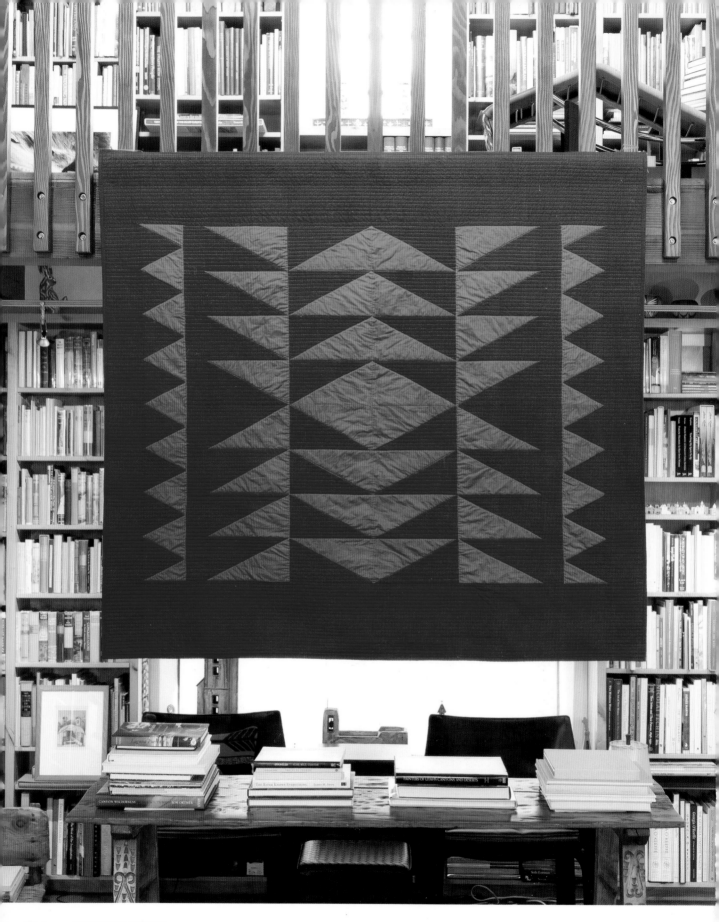